Marvel Studios'
Avengers: Infinity War

Based on the Screenplay by
Christopher Markus and Stephen McFeely
Story by Stan Lee

Produced by Kevin Feige, p.g.a.
Directed by Anthony and Joe Russo

Level 5

Retold by Mary Tomalin

Series Editors: Andy Hopkins and Jocelyn Potter

T0345366

Pearson Education Limited

KAO Two

KAO Park, Harlow,

Essex, CM17 9NA, England

and Associated Companies throughout the world.

ISBN: 978-1-2923-4752-3

This edition first published by Pearson Education Ltd 2018

1 3 5 7 9 10 8 6 4 2

© 2021 MARVEL

Set in 9pt/14pt Xenois Slab Pro

Printed by Neografia, Slovakia

Published by Pearson Education Limited

For a complete list of the titles available in the Pearson English Readers series, visit
www.pearsonenglishreaders.com.
Alternatively, write to your local Pearson Education office or
to Pearson English Readers Marketing Department,
Pearson Education, KAO Two, KAO Park, Harlow, Essex, CM17 9NA

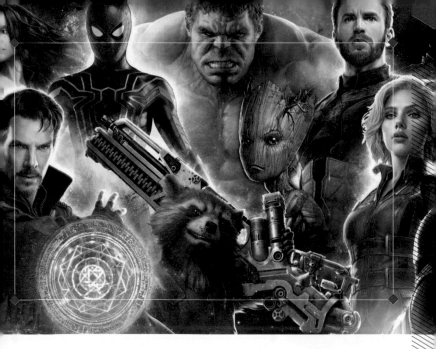

Contents

	page
Who's Who?	iv
Introduction	vii
Chapter 1: Thanos's Plans	1
Chapter 2: The Attack on New York	8
Chapter 3: To the Rescue	25
Chapter 4: The Promise	36
Chapter 5: Avengers—Together Again	42
Chapter 6: The Price of Love	49
Chapter 7: Love and Loss	56
Chapter 8: The Battle of Wakanda	64
Chapter 9: The Battle of Titan	74
Chapter 10: Victory	85
Activities	94
Word List	103

Who's Who?

Thanos

Thanos—also known as the Titan, after the planet where he was born—is an extremely cruel and powerful warlord, with superhuman strength and abilities. He was forced to leave Titan, and now has an evil plan for the rest of the universe.

Children of Thanos

Thanos adopted children from different worlds and trained them to be killers to increase his strength. **Ebony Maw** is a talented sorcerer. **Cull Obsidian** is enormously strong. **Proxima Midnight** uses a powerful spear. **Corvus Glaive** is a skillful fighter.

Dr. Stephen Strange / Doctor Strange

Dr. Stephen Strange trained as a sorcerer after an accident ended his work with patients. As Doctor Strange, he leads a group of sorcerers, including his assistant, **Wong**. From a base in New York, they protect Earth from magical attacks.

Thor

Thor, the God of Thunder, was King of Asgard before his world was destroyed. He has superhuman strength, although his powerful hammer, Mjolnir, has been destroyed. He has a difficult relationship with his brother **Loki**, who enjoys playing with people's minds.

Steve Rogers / Captain America

Rogers was given superpowers by the U.S. government and became Captain America. After a heroic plane crash in the Arctic, he was unconscious for sixty-six years before becoming an Avenger.

Tony Stark / Iron Man

Stark is a scientist and Avenger. His special suit, supported by a computer system called FRIDAY, gives him superhuman powers. His technology company is now run by his girlfriend, **Pepper Potts**.

Natasha Romanoff / Black Widow

Natasha was trained by the Russian security service as a spy and killer. After she was persuaded to join the U.S. agency S.H.I.E.L.D., she became an extremely skillful fighter for the Avengers.

Bruce Banner / Hulk

Banner is a smart scientist who becomes an enormous, violent creature when he is angry. He is a valued member of the Avengers team, but is increasingly unwilling to change into Hulk.

Wanda Maximoff / Scarlet Witch and Vision

Wanda was given superpowers by an evil organization called Hydra, but later joined the Avengers. Vision is an android created by Stark and Banner.

Peter Parker / Spider-Man

Parker is a teenager who originally developed superpowers and fought crime in New York City. He was then persuaded by Stark to fight with him in a war between different teams of Avengers.

T'Challa / Black Panther

T'Challa is the king of the African country Wakanda. His superpowers give him the abilities of a big cat. His sister **Shuri** is a scientist. **Okoye** is the head of the Wakandan guards.

Peter Quill / Star-Lord

Quill, half human and half Celestial, was kidnapped from Earth by Ravagers and trained in criminal behavior. He now leads a strange team known as the Guardians of the Galaxy.

Drax, Mantis, Rocket, and Groot

Drax is a fighter. Mantis changes people's feelings through touch. Rocket is an engineer with superpowers. Groot can grow things from his body. They are the Guardians of the Galaxy.

Gamora

Gamora was kidnapped and adopted by Thanos, who trained her to be a killer. She was his favorite child, but eventually turned against him. She has now joined the Guardians of the Galaxy.

Nebula

Nebula was also kidnapped by Thanos and taught to be a killer. When she lost training fights with her sister Gamora, Thanos changed parts of her body. She hated Gamora for never letting her win.

Eitri

Eitri is the keeper of the only remaining forge on the star of Nidavellir. His people were friends of the Asgardians and made Thor's hammer, Mjolnir, but Nidavellir has suffered a terrible defeat.

Introduction

Staring down into the hole, the sorcerers saw a middle-aged man lying on his back. Bruce Banner had changed from Hulk back to his human form. Transported by the Bifrost, he had crashed through the roof of the building. Banner wore pants, but there was nothing on his top half, and he was groaning loudly.

"Thanos is coming! He's coming!" he whispered, in a voice filled with terror.

The two sorcerers looked at each other.

"Who?" asked Doctor Strange.

Thanos, a cruel warlord from the planet Titan, is searching the universe for the Infinity Stones. They came into existence when the universe began, and each Stone controls a different way the universe works. There are six Infinity Stones, and each one is enormously powerful:

The red **Reality Stone** can change reality and make things appear completely different.

The green **Time Stone** allows its user to make time go backward or forward.

The blue **Space Stone** is hidden inside a crystal called the Tesseract. Its user can travel through portals to different parts of the universe.

The purple **Power Stone** gives its user enormous energy to create or destroy.

The yellow **Mind Stone** can be used to control the minds of others. It was also used to create an android called Vision.

The orange **Soul Stone** allows its user to control people's souls, and gives the user control over all life in the universe.

If Thanos gets all six Infinity Stones, he will become the most powerful being in the universe, and will then be able to achieve his unimaginably evil goal. At the start of the book, the warlord has the Power Stone, and is already very powerful. Super heroes from different parts of the galaxy unite to stop him collecting the other five Stones.

The Avengers are a group of super heroes who have fought many battles to protect Earth. Among them are the wealthy inventor Tony Stark, and the God of Thunder, Thor, from the realm of Asgard. Black Panther is king of the technologically advanced African country Wakanda. Like the other great fighters, he is prepared for the worst—and it is coming.

The Guardians of the Galaxy are a group of super heroes who used to be criminals. Now, they work together to protect the galaxy from alien attacks. The super heroes are willing to give their lives. But even if they do, is this enough to save the universe?

Marvel Studios' Avengers: Infinity War (2018) is one of the most successful movies of all time. It is the 19th film in the Marvel Cinematic Universe, an imaginary universe based on the adventures of super heroes in Marvel Comics. The movie follows the events that take place in *Marvel Studios' Captain America: Civil War*, *Marvel Studios' Black Panther*, and *Marvel Studios' Thor: Ragnarok*. The action takes place on Earth and other planets. Robert Downey Jr. stars as Iron Man, Chris Hemsworth plays Thor, Scarlett Johansson stars as Black Widow, and Chadwick Boseman plays Black Panther. The film was widely praised for its actors' performances and action scenes, and is one of the most expensive movies ever made. *Marvel Studios' Avengers: Endgame* (2019) follows *Avengers: Infinity War*, and is also a Pearson English Reader.

All through history, there are stories of magical stones and jewels that give their possessors great power. There are, for example, Japanese stories about jewels that gave their possessors control of the tides, and in Hindu stories possession of the jewel Symantaka protected lands from floods and other disasters. *Avengers: Infinity War* is also in the great tradition of stories in which heroes battle against evil—but can they win?

Thanos's Plans

Deep in space, far, far away from Earth, a spaceship was sending out a signal for help.

"This is the Asgardian spaceship, the *Statesman*. We are under attack. I repeat, we are under attack. The engines are dead, our systems are failing. We are requesting help from any spaceship near us. We are Asgardian families, we have very few soldiers. We are *not* a warship."

The speaker sounded frightened—even desperate. An enormous spaceship was firing missiles at the *Statesman*. Inside the *Statesman*, fires were burning, and dead and wounded people lay everywhere.

Thor, who was the king of the realm of Asgard and the Asgardian God of Thunder, was on the ship with his younger brother Loki. Loki, also a god, had fought against his brother in the past, and had even been King of Asgard for a time. But now they were on the same side. They had left Asgard after their world had been destroyed, and almost all its people had died in a terrible war. The Asgardians who were still alive were on the spaceship. Thor had decided to take them to Earth, and make a new home there. But even this hope was gone now.

The much larger spaceship was the *Sanctuary II*, and was the base of Thanos, a warlord from the planet Titan. Soon, Ebony Maw, one of Thanos's best fighters, was walking through the *Statesman*, carefully stepping over the bodies.

"Hear me and be glad. You are lucky to be saved by the great Titan," Ebony Maw said calmly in a thin, high voice. "You may think this is suffering. No—it is a new beginning. As a result of your deaths, there will be more balance in the universe."

He pressed his hands together; his long fingers were as pale as his face. He was a tall, frightening alien in a tight, gray suit and heavy boots. He had gray skin, a long face with a flat nose, and thin, white hair.

There were other fighters with him. They had been adopted by Thanos as children, and were known as the "Children of Thanos." Thanos had trained them to be killers. Proxima Midnight wore black, and her eyes, deep in her head, shone with hatred. Cull Obsidian was enormous, with a skin like a snake's. Corvus Glaive looked small and thin beside him, but carried a spear with a blade at both ends. Only Proxima Midnight looked mostly human.

Dark-haired Loki was a prisoner on the spaceship, but was unharmed. He was watching a figure who stood looking out of a window. It was Thanos himself. The Titan was enormous and frighteningly strong. He was wearing battle armor, and his pale purple skin looked like leather. Beneath his helmet, his eyes were as cold as death. His large chin had long lines on it. Those who saw him could only feel terror.

He turned around now, and spoke in a deep voice that sounded strangely kind. "I know how it feels to lose—when you feel so desperately that you're right, but then you fail."

Thor was lying wounded on the ground. Thanos picked him up by the neck, and the god groaned.

"Why fear death?" Thanos continued. "It always comes to you in the end." He walked toward Loki as he spoke. "It's here now. Or should I say, *I am?*"

He lifted Thor's fair-haired, bearded head like a toy. The god had lost one eye in a previous battle. Blood came from his mouth.

"You talk too much," he managed to say.

Thanos held up his left hand to show Loki the Infinity Gauntlet that covered it. It was a glove with spaces in it for six extremely powerful Stones. They were called Infinity Stones, and each Stone could control the universe in a different way. One Stone was already in the gauntlet—the pale purple Power Stone.

Thanos had one purpose in life—to control the whole universe. He was searching for the other five Infinity Stones. This was the reason he had attacked the *Statesman*. Thanos knew that Loki had the Tesseract, a crystal that contained the Space Stone. Loki had once fought for Thanos, and had promised to obtain the Tesseract for him. But the Avengers had prevented Loki from getting it, and Thor had taken his brother and the Tesseract to Asgard.

Now, Thanos looked at him, and smiled. "Give me the Tesseract. Or your brother's head. Choose. Which do you prefer?"

The Children of Thanos raised their weapons threateningly as he spoke.

Loki thought about it. "Kill him."

Thanos was surprised, but bent down and placed the gauntlet on Thor's forehead. The Power Stone shone brightly, and Thor screamed—and screamed. The Titan watched Loki expectantly as he did this. After only a few moments of Thor's screams, his pain was too much, even for Loki.

"All right, stop!" he shouted.

Thanos removed his hand.

"We don't have the Tesseract," Thor groaned. "It was destroyed on Asgard."

This wasn't true, but he was desperate for Thanos not to possess the Stone. He watched in horror as Loki raised his right hand, and the Tesseract appeared in it. The blue light of the Stone shone inside the crystal. Thanos smiled with pleasure.

"You really are the worst brother," Thor said, disgusted.

Loki walked toward Thanos, holding up the Tesseract. Always confident, he looked at Thor and said, "I promise you, brother, the sun will shine again."

"You're wrong, Asgardian," said Thanos.

Loki lifted a finger to correct him. "Well, that's *one* mistake—I'm not Asgardian. And ... We have a Hulk."

As he said the word "Hulk," Loki dropped the Tesseract, and dived toward Thor. He pulled his brother away from Thanos just as an enormous figure ran roaring from the side of the ship and jumped on the Titan. It was Hulk, a very large, strong creature with green skin. It was hard to believe that he was also a very smart scientist called Bruce Banner. Because of an accident in a laboratory, Banner changed into Hulk when he became very angry or excited. Hulk had fought with a group of super heroes called the Avengers, and was on the spaceship because he had helped the Asgardians in their fight to save their planet.

Hulk hit the surprised Titan again and again. He pushed him until he was against the wall of the ship, and then hit him once more. Cull Obsidian moved to help his father, but Ebony Maw lifted a hand to stop him.

"Let him have his fun," Ebony Maw said calmly. He had no doubt that Thanos would win. He was right. Thanos put his hands on Hulk's great arms. There was an expression of surprise and fear on the creature's green face as the Titan slowly removed Hulk's hands from his shoulders. The two enormous figures began fighting again. But this time, Thanos picked Hulk up, held him over his head, and threw him to the ground, unconscious.

While the Titan stood there, Thor came behind him and hit him with a metal bar. Thanos turned, and kicked Thor across the floor. Ebony Maw moved into action. He was able to lift and move things using his mental

powers. Now, he raised a hand, and some twisted pieces of metal flew across the room. They wrapped themselves around the Asgardian so he couldn't move.

The Asgardian gatekeeper Heimdall was lying wounded on the floor. On Asgard, he had had the important job of guarding the Bifrost Bridge. The Bifrost was a bridge of energy, creating portals that could transport people and objects over great distances in almost no time. Now, making a great effort, Heimdall lifted his right hand.

"Allfathers ... let the dark magic move through me one last ... time," he prayed.

The shining beam of the Bifrost filled the ship. It shone down on Hulk, its lovely colors covering him. He flew up into the beam, and disappeared. The Bifrost carried him far away, deep into space.

"That was a mistake," said Thanos, extremely angry. Taking Corvus Glaive's spear, he pushed it deep into the Asgardian's chest. But Heimdall, as he died, was smiling. He had saved Hulk.

"You're going to die for that, Thanos!" cried Thor, unable to believe he had lost his friend.

Ebony Maw made a movement with his wrist, and a piece of metal wrapped itself around Thor's mouth.

"*Shh*," Ebony Maw said. Then, kneeling in front of Thanos, he offered his father the Tesseract. "No other being has ever had the strength to possess not one but *two* Infinity Stones. The universe will soon be yours."

It shone down on Hulk, its lovely colors covering him.

Thanos had waited a long time for this moment. He removed his helmet and chest armor. Then, holding the Tesseract in one enormous hand, he closed his hand tightly. When he opened it, the Space Stone, surrounded by tiny pieces of crystal, shone with a bright, blue light. He rolled the Stone between his fingers, enjoying the feeling of it, then placed it next to the Power Stone in his gauntlet.

"*Aaah!*" he shouted, as a great blast of energy shook him. "There are two more Stones on Earth. Find them, my children, and bring them to me," he said slowly.

His children knelt in front of him.

"Father, we will not fail you," Proxima Midnight said.

Loki suddenly appeared from the shadows. "If you're going to Earth, you might want a guide. I have some experience in that area," he said, smiling.

"If you think failure is experience," Thanos replied.

"I consider that *experience* is experience," Loki replied, walking toward him. "Great Thanos ... I ... Loki ... Prince of Asgard ... promise to be loyal to you forever."

He looked at Thor for a moment as he spoke, and Thor saw that his brother was hiding a knife in his left hand. Moving at great speed, Loki raised the knife to stab Thanos. But he was shocked to find his arm frozen in mid-air. The blue energy of the Space Stone flowed from the knife and down his arm.

"Forever? You should choose your words more carefully," Thanos said, twisting the knife out of Loki's hand. He lifted the god up, and squeezed his throat. Loki struggled and kicked, unable to breathe. Thanos tightened his hand, pure cruelty in his smile. Loki's bones cracked, and he stopped kicking.

"No!" Thor screamed through the metal around his mouth.

Thanos dropped his brother's body in front of him. Then, he raised his gauntleted hand. Pale purple fires appeared. The Children of Thanos moved to stand around him. The blue Space Stone shone brightly, and they all disappeared.

Now that Ebony Maw was gone, the metal holding Thor fell off him, and he moved on his hands and knees toward Loki's body. As the fires burned around him, the God of Thunder lay his head down on his brother's chest, tears running down his face. Loki had often deceived him, and they had fought each other in battle. But despite this, Thor had loved him deeply.

Thanos hadn't finished. The *Sanctuary II* fired for the last time on the *Statesman*, and the small spaceship exploded. The warlord's spaceship disappeared. It had done its work. But Hulk continued his journey through deep space, carried to Earth by the Bifrost. Flying impossibly fast, he sped past stars, planets, and moons. He reached the planet Earth, and was transported toward New York.

"No!" Thor screamed through the metal around his mouth.

The Attack on New York

In a large and beautiful old house in New York's Greenwich Village, two men were walking down some wide stairs to the hall on the ground floor. Only a few people knew the real name of the house—the *Sanctum Sanctorum*. It was the home of the most powerful sorcerer in the universe, Doctor Strange. He led a group of sorcerers who protected Earth from magical attacks. Doctor Strange was with his friend and assistant, Wong. They were discussing what to have for lunch.

"Seriously? You don't have any money?" Doctor Strange asked.

"Money is not important in the spiritual world," Wong replied.

"I'll tell the guys at the café."

"Oh, wait, wait, I think I have some," Wong said, pulling out a few small notes from his pocket.

"What do you want?" inquired Doctor Strange.

"I'd be happy with a sandwich."

Suddenly, a loud crash interrupted the men's conversation, and they fell on their knees with their hands over their heads to protect themselves. They turned around and saw a beam of light shining down from the roof. There was a large hole in the stairs, and they ran toward it. A red cloak appeared around Doctor Strange's shoulders, and Wong created bright, magical circles of energy. The beam of light disappeared.

Staring down into the hole, the sorcerers saw a middle-aged man lying on his back. Bruce Banner had changed from Hulk back to his human form. Transported by the Bifrost, he had crashed through the roof of the building. Banner wore pants, but there was nothing on his top half, and he was groaning loudly.

"Thanos is coming! He's coming!" he whispered, in a voice filled with terror.

The two men looked at each other.

"Who?" asked Doctor Strange.

In another part of New York, Tony Stark and his girlfriend, Pepper Potts, were walking by the river in Central Park. It was a sunny spring day, and the couple was enjoying their time away from work. Stark was an extraordinary man. An extremely wealthy industrialist, he was also one of the world's greatest scientists and inventors. He had created an armored suit that had very advanced technology, and could fire missiles and fly. Using the suit, Stark had helped to save Earth from its enemies a number of times, and he was famous as the super hero Iron Man.

Pepper Potts was the head of Stark's company, Stark Industries. The couple loved each other deeply, and planned to get married. Nobody noticed them now as they walked in the park together.

Stark turned to look at Pepper. "Last night I dreamed we had a kid. And when I woke up, I thought it was real," he said, excitement in his voice.

"So you woke up and thought that we were expecting a baby? No!" Pepper said.

Stark felt disappointed. He had hoped Pepper would love the idea of having a child.

"If you wanted to have a kid, you wouldn't have *that*," Pepper said, touching the shiny, metal Arc Reactor on his chest, which provided all the energy for Stark's Iron Man suit.

Stark tried to explain that it was necessary for their protection. "There might be something scary in the closet, instead of, you know ..."

"Shirts." Pepper looked at her boyfriend lovingly. "You should have *shirts* in your closet."

She wanted a life in which the man she loved was not in danger.

"You know what there should be? No more surprises," Stark said. "We're going to have a nice dinner tonight. People need to know about our wedding plans. And we should have no more surprises. Ever. I should promise you."

"Yes," Pepper said, laughing, hoping he meant his words.

The couple were gently kissing when a voice came from behind them.

"Tony Stark, I'm Doctor Strange. I need you to come with me. Oh, yes, and congratulations on your wedding plans."

They turned around to see a spinning circle of orange light hanging in the air. It was a portal, and Doctor Strange stepped out of it wearing his blue sorcerer's suit and red cloak. Shocked, the couple held each other's hands protectively.

"We need your help. It's not an exaggeration to say the universe is in great danger," Doctor Strange said urgently.

"And who's 'we'?" Stark asked in disbelief. He had no idea who this man was.

Another man appeared from the portal. It was Bruce Banner, and Stark knew *him* well. They hadn't seen each other for a long time, and Stark was very glad to see him now.

"Hey, Tony!" Banner said.

"Bruce. You O.K.?"

Looking frightened, Banner put his arms around his friend. Stark stared at Doctor Strange. If Banner was scared, maybe the universe really *was* in danger.

In the library of the *Sanctum Sanctorum,* tiny stars were hanging in the air. Wong and Doctor Strange were using magic to show Stark and Banner the universe. The scientists, who had never seen this kind of magic before, were listening carefully.

"When the universe began, there was nothing," Wong said. He waved his hands, and six shining Stones of different colors appeared. "Then, *bang!* The Big Bang sent six crystals flying across the universe. They are Infinity Stones. Each Stone can be used to control the universe in a different way."

Doctor Strange named the Stones, and they each lit up as he mentioned them. "Space. Reality. Power. Soul. Mind." Looking down, Doctor Strange touched a piece of jewelry hanging from his neck. Sorcerers called it the "Eye of Agamotto," and the Time Stone was inside it. "And Time," he said.

He waved his hands, and the Eye opened to show a shining, green Stone. Stark felt much more respect for Doctor Strange now that he knew the sorcerer possessed the Time Stone. Only someone very powerful could use an Infinity Stone. But there was a lot more that he wanted to know.

"What was the name of this guy you talked about?" he asked.

"Thanos," Banner replied. He had seen terrible things on the *Statesman,* and it showed in his eyes. "He's really evil, Tony. He attacks planets, takes what he wants, and kills half the population. You know that attack on New York? That was *him.*"

Five years ago, Loki and an army of aliens—Chitauri, in service to Thanos—had tried to take New York. At the end of the great battle, Stark

They are Infinity Stones. Each Stone can be used to control the universe in a different way.

had saved the planet by destroying the Chitauri command center. At the time, nobody knew that the attack was part of an agreement between Loki and Thanos.

"How much time do we have?" Stark asked.

"I've no idea. Thanos has the Power and Space Stones." Banner followed Stark as he walked around the room. "He's already the strongest creature in the whole universe," the scientist said quietly. "If he gets all six Stones, Tony ..."

Doctor Strange finished his sentence: "He can destroy life in a way that's never happened before."

Hearing this, Stark had a simple answer. "If Thanos needs all six Stones, why don't we just destroy the Time Stone?"

Doctor Strange shook his head. "That can't be done."

"We promised to protect the Time Stone with our lives," Wong explained.

"And I promised myself not to eat milk and cheese, but then they named an ice cream after me," Stark replied.

"I know the one," Doctor Strange said. "It could be better."

"It's not our favorite," Wong added.

"Listen—things change," Stark said, becoming serious again. *The best solution is definitely to destroy the Time Stone*, he thought.

But Doctor Strange wouldn't change his mind. "This Stone may be the best chance we have against Thanos," he said firmly.

"And it could be *his* best chance against *us*."

"If we don't do our job," Doctor Strange replied.

"What *is* your job exactly?"

Doctor Strange paused, and then said with a small smile, "Protecting your reality!" He knew Stark had no idea of the important magical work that he and his group of sorcerers did to protect Earth.

Banner interrupted the two men. They were both extremely powerful, and had very high opinions of themselves. But this was no time to argue—they needed to work together. Thanos had to be prevented from finding the Stones.

"The fact is that we have this Stone. We know where it is," Banner said. "Vision is out there somewhere with the Mind Stone, and we have to find him *now*."

Stark folded his arms over his chest, thinking hard. Vision was an android that he had created with the help of Banner, using very advanced technology. The Mind Stone had been placed in Vison's forehead, and it had brought him to life. When this happened, Vision made a promise that he would fight to protect Earth. But Vision himself now needed protection.

"That's a problem," Stark said. "Two weeks ago, Vision turned off his radio receiver. I can't find him."

"*What?*" shouted Banner. One thing was clear—to protect the Mind Stone, they *had* to find Vision.

"Who could find him?" Doctor Strange asked.

Stark thought for a moment. "Probably Steve Rogers … maybe. But …"

He sighed. Steve Rogers, who was also the super hero Captain America, was the last person on Earth he wanted to see. But Banner was delighted to hear Captain America's name. His friend "Cap" was the world's first super hero and they needed his help.

"Call him," he said.

"It's not so easy. God, I haven't seen you for a long time, have I?" Stark said.

Stark, Rogers, Banner, and Vision had been part of a group of extraordinary men and women with superpowers. The group was known as the Avengers, and their purpose was to protect Earth. They had saved the planet from attack a number of times, but there had been strong disagreements and even battles between them, and the group had split in two. Stark was the leader of the group that was happy to work with governments. The other group had refused to do this—they believed it was important to be independent. Rogers was the leader of this group, and governments considered it to be a group of criminals. As a result, Stark and Rogers hadn't seen each other for two years. Stark felt partly responsible for the break-up, but there was no time now to explain how it had all happened.

"The Avengers broke up. We're finished," Stark informed Banner.

This was a surprise to the scientist, who had been out of contact with the other super heroes for some time.

"Thanos is coming. It doesn't matter who you're talking to or not."

"Broke up? Like a band? Like the Beatles?" Banner asked, puzzled. The Avengers had worked so well together.

"Cap and I aren't speaking to each other."

"Tony, listen to me," Banner said forcefully. "Thor's dead. Thanos is coming. It doesn't matter who you're talking to or not."

Knowing Banner was right, Stark stepped away from the group, and took a small cell phone out of his pocket. There was only one number on it—Rogers's number. He had never used the phone, but then nothing like this had ever happened before. He was just starting to make the phone call when he stopped. There was a low, electronic noise coming from somewhere, and the furniture was shaking slightly. He turned, and saw that Doctor Strange's hair was moving slightly.

"Doc, are you moving your hair?" he asked.

"Not at the moment, no," Doctor Strange replied.

The four men looked up at the hole in the roof that the Bifrost had made as it entered. Above it, objects were flying past in the air. They turned to look out the large front door—people were running past, screaming. Clearly, something bad was happening. They went out onto the street, and found an extraordinary scene. The traffic had stopped, and everyone was running in the same direction. Car alarms were sounding.

Stark put on his glasses. They contained technology that allowed him to contact FRIDAY, a computer system he had created to use with his Iron Man armor.

"FRIDAY, what's happening?" he demanded.

"Not sure. I'm working on it," a woman's voice replied.

Doctor Strange, just behind Stark, had magical rings of energy around his arms.

"Hey, you might want to put that Time Stone in your back pocket, Doc!" Stark shouted.

"I might want to *use* it," the sorcerer replied angrily.

They walked to the next street. Now, the electronic sound was much louder. Just above the street, there was an enormous spaceship in the shape of a ring. It didn't look like anything on Earth, and could only mean one thing. There was no time left. Thanos had arrived.

A short distance away, on Queensboro Bridge, a bus was taking teenagers into Manhattan on a school trip. On the bus was Peter Parker, who was secretly the super hero Spider-Man. He used his unusual powers to fight crime in New York, while still attending school. He had fought with the Avengers, and Stark had improved his Spider-Man suit with new technology. Parker wanted more than anything to become a real Avenger.

The teenager was asleep on the bus when the tiny hairs on his arms suddenly stood up. He woke, and looked at his arms in surprise. When this happened, it always meant danger. Looking out the window, he was amazed to see an enormous spaceship. *This is why I'm feeling scared. I need to act fast,* Parker thought. His friend, Ned, was in the seat in front of him, and Parker shook his shoulder.

"Ned, hey, I need you to do something. I have to get out of here. No one must see me leave."

Looking over Parker's shoulder, Ned's eyes widened in fear.

"Oh, my God! We're all going to die! There's a spaceship!" he cried.

He got up, and ran to the back of the bus. Everyone followed him, screaming. Parker took out his web shooter, and put it on his wrist. It

They had no idea that Parker was outside the bus, holding onto it.

made webs and web lines that could fasten onto anything. He pressed a button, and it shot a web line out to the emergency window on the other side of the bus. The teenager pulled, and when the window opened, he jumped out.

"What's the matter with you kids? Haven't you ever seen a spaceship before?" asked the bus driver as the students screamed in terror.

They had no idea that Parker was outside the bus, holding onto it. He reached in and seized his bag, which contained his Spider-Man suit. Using the web lines, with astonishing speed, he swung under the bridge, over the river, and toward the spaceship.

Below the spaceship, the traffic had stopped, and cars had crashed into each other.

"FRIDAY!" shouted Iron Man, "Get everyone south of 43rd Street off the streets. Call the police and fire department!"

"Will do," replied FRIDAY.

A pale blue beam of energy came down from the ship just ten meters in front of the four super heroes. Two figures appeared, one tall and thin, the other enormous. Unafraid, the super heroes began walking slowly toward the aliens. They stopped when Ebony Maw started speaking.

"Hear me, and be happy," Ebony Maw said in his high voice. "The Children of Thanos will kill you today. Be glad that your lives are ..."

"I'm sorry, Earth is closed today. You'd better get out of here," interrupted Stark.

"Stone keeper, does this foolish animal speak for you?" Ebony Maw said to Doctor Strange, ignoring Stark. He already knew that the sorcerer had the Time Stone, and the alien was in New York with one purpose only—to bring the Stone to Thanos.

"Certainly not. I speak for myself. Get off this city and off this planet!" Doctor Strange replied. He and Wong walked forward, making movements with their arms. Powerful, magical shields in the form of bright circles of energy appeared in front of them.

"He means, get out of here, fish face!" Stark shouted.

"He makes me feel tired. Bring me the Stone," Ebony Maw said in his own language to Cull Obsidian.

The enormous creature made a low, animal sound, and started walking toward the super heroes, dragging a frightening-looking hammer along the ground.

Stark turned to Banner, a small smile on his face. "Banner, do you want to fight?"

"No, not really, but when do I ever get what I want?" Banner answered.

He closed his eyes, and concentrated. Previously, when he did this, he immediately changed into Hulk, but this time nothing happened. Banner's neck turned green, and that was all.

"It's been some time, old friend," Stark said sympathetically. "It's good to have you here."

"I just ... I need to concentrate for one second," Banner told him.

Banner made a terrible face. Again, nothing happened. Cull Obsidian was getting closer.

"Where's Hulk?" Stark asked, worried.

"I don't know," Banner replied, very embarrassed now.

He gave a loud cry, but again, nothing happened. Doctor Strange turned to look at him.

"You're embarrassing me in front of these guys," Stark said in a low voice.

Banner felt terrible. "I'm sorry, Tony—either I can't, or he won't," he said.

"It's O.K. Make sure he's O.K.," Stark said to Wong.

"Will do," Wong answered.

As Cull Obsidian ran toward them, roaring, Stark pulled at two cords on his T-shirt. Then, he touched his Arc Reactor, and started walking forward. In seconds, a red and gold suit of armor covered his body. He took off his glasses, and a helmet covered his head. Stark was now Iron Man. Cull Obsidian swung his hammer down. Iron Man raised his arm, and a shield appeared that protected him. He fired missiles that struck Cull Obsidian, throwing him toward Ebony Maw. Ebony Maw raised a hand, and the alien was thrown into some cars.

Ebony Maw's intention was to remove all the fighters except Doctor Strange. He raised his hand again, and Iron Man was thrown high in the air. With another wave of his hand, the alien sent trees and debris flying toward the group. Wong immediately put up a shield.

"Doctor Banner, if the rest of your green friend won't be joining us ..." Doctor Strange said.

He didn't finish his sentence, but the next thing Banner knew, he was lying on the ground in a park near the street. The sorcerer had transported him there through a portal. The back end of a taxi, cut in half as the portal closed, just missed him.

Iron Man returned to the fight. "We have to get that Stone out of here now," he told Doctor Strange.

"It stays with me," Doctor Strange said firmly.

Iron Man started flying through the objects thrown by Ebony Maw. Then, he met Cull Obsidian's hammer, and was thrown through a building and into the park. He landed against a tree, making a hole in the ground. Banner ran to his fallen friend.

"Tony, are you O.K.? How are we doing? Good? Bad?" he asked.

"Really, really good. Really good. Do you plan to help?" Iron Man said calmly, though he didn't feel calm at all.

"I'm trying. Hulk won't come out," Banner said desperately.

As he spoke, Cull Obsidian appeared, and threw his hammer at them. Iron Man pushed Banner out of the way just in time. He blasted Cull Obsidian with energy beams from his gloved hands, but the alien easily blocked them with his shield.

Banner was still trying to get Hulk to appear. "Come on, Hulk, what are you doing to me?" he demanded. He started hitting his face.

"Come out! Come out! Come out!" he shouted.

Half of Banner's face started changing into Hulk. Banner roared "No!" in Hulk's voice, before changing back into himself again. He fell to the ground, exhausted.

"What do you mean, no?" he cried angrily.

The battle between Iron Man and Cull Obsidian continued. The terrible creature knocked Iron Man to the ground, and raised his hammer.

"Hey, man!" a voice said. "What's happening, Mr. Stark?"

It was Spider-Man, and he was holding the hammer from below.

Cull Obsidian swung his hammer down. Iron Man raised his arm, and a shield appeared that protected him.

"Kid! Where did you come from?" asked Iron Man, astonished. The teenager had saved his life.

"I was on a school trip."

As Spider-Man spoke, Cull Obsidian seized him, and threw him across the park. But using a web line, the young hero swung back across the park, and returned to the fight.

"What's this guy's problem, Mr. Stark?" he asked. He seemed to feel no fear.

"He's from space. He came here to steal something from a sorcerer," Iron Man said from inside his armored suit.

Before Spider-Man could say that that sounded amazing, Cull Obsidian threw a car at his head. This was definitely not the school trip Peter Parker had imagined when he woke up that morning.

Several streets away, Doctor Strange and Wong were still fighting Ebony Maw. The alien threw Wong across the street, knocking him unconscious. Doctor Strange created a band of energy that wrapped itself around Ebony Maw's hands. But the Child of Thanos rose in the air, and pulled on the line until the sorcerer was upside-down, high against the wall of a building.

"Your powers are amusing. You must be popular with children," Ebony Maw said in his cold voice, floating in the air near him.

Bricks fell on him from above, covering most of his body.

"Your powers are amusing. You must be popular with children," Ebony Maw said in his cold voice, floating in the air near him. The Time Stone was shining brightly on Doctor Strange's chest, and the alien put out his hand to take it. Then, he screamed in pain as it burned his hands.

"It's a simple spell, but unbreakable," Doctor Strange said confidently.

Ebony Maw's eyes narrowed. "Then I'll take it off your dead body," he said, and threw Doctor Strange down to the street below.

The sorcerer rolled over, jumped to his feet, and began to make movements to open the Eye of Agamotto. But using his extraordinary powers, Ebony Maw brought metal pipes out of the ground. They wrapped themselves tightly around Doctor Strange's body and neck. Doctor Strange groaned as he struggled to escape.

"You'll find it difficult to remove a dead man's spell," he managed to say. But the pipes got tighter and tighter, and it was hard for him to breathe.

The sorcerer fell to the ground unconscious, and Ebony Maw lifted the part of the sidewalk that had Doctor Strange on it up into the air. The alien started to move along the street, followed by Doctor Strange. But the sorcerer's cloak had magical powers. It pulled Doctor Strange free of the pipes, and flew him away from the alien.

"No!" Ebony Maw screamed.

In the park, as Iron Man and Cull Obsidian were battling with each other, Iron Man was astonished to see Doctor Strange flying through the air, unconscious, with his cloak guiding him.

"Kid, that's the sorcerer," Iron Man shouted to Spider-Man. "Do something!"

The teenager spun around, amazed. He had fought with the Avengers, and seen many extraordinary things, but nothing like this. A magic cloak was carrying a sorcerer through a New York park.

"Will do!" he shouted.

Ebony Maw was chasing Doctor Strange through Manhattan, so Spider-Man followed him. The alien started bending street poles, and one of them pulled the sorcerer's cloak from under him. Using his web lines, Spider-Man caught Doctor Strange before he hit the sidewalk.

Just then, a blue beam of light shone down from the spaceship onto Doctor Strange, and the sorcerer, his cloak, and Spider-Man began to float upward. Spider-Man thought this was amazing, but very scary. Luckily, his suit had a radio connection to Iron Man.

"Uh, Mr. Stark, I'm being beamed up," he radioed.

"Wait a minute, kid," Iron Man shouted. He wasn't winning the fight against Cull Obsidian. Now, the creature's hammer separated into two parts, and pinned him to the ground. Cull Obsidian jumped high in the air toward him, holding an enormous blade. It looked like the end of the super hero. But instead, the alien passed through a shining portal into a scene of mountains and snow. He turned around, roaring, and started to jump through the portal back into the park. But he didn't get through. Wong, who had created the portal, had quickly closed it. The magical door cut off one of Cull Obsidian's hands as it closed, and the hand rolled toward Banner. He kicked it away, looking disgusted.

"Wong, you're invited to my wedding," Iron Man said gratefully.

He had got free of the hammer, and now he shot up toward the spaceship, powered by small jets of energy from his gloves and boots. The ship was much higher in the sky now. He knew that if Spider-Man reached it, he would soon be unable to breathe. The boy hero needed help.

"Unlock 17-A!" Iron Man ordered FRIDAY. Immediately, at great speed, a pod flew from the Avengers building, in the north of New York state, up toward the spaceship.

While all this was happening, Spider-Man had reached the ship and was climbing up one side of it. Inside, Ebony Maw had arrived, too, and was inside, walking toward the controls. Doctor Strange, still unconscious, floated behind him. Ebony Maw put his hands on the controls, and prepared to leave Earth.

"Pete, let yourself drop. I'm going to catch you," Iron Man radioed.

"But you said save the sorcerer!" Spider-Man shouted, then a moment later said, "I can't breathe!"

"You're too high up. There's no air there," Iron Man told him.

The teenager became unconscious, and started falling through the air. The pod from the Avengers building reached him just in time. It fastened itself to him and changed into a metal Spider-Man spacesuit. When Parker recovered consciousness, he couldn't believe it—he was in a spacesuit, and could breathe again. How had Iron Man done it? He landed on the underside of the spaceship, and managed to stand up. Like a spider, the spacesuit could fasten itself to things.

"Mr. Stark, it smells like a new car in here," he said excitedly.

Iron Man, who had reached the spaceship, saw him and smiled. *The boy deserves to be an Avenger*, he thought.

"Have a good journey, kid. FRIDAY, send him home," he said, thankful he had saved the teenager's life.

A parachute opened from the spacesuit, and pulled Spider-Man away from the ship.

"*No!*" cried Spider-Man.

Iron Man fired an energy beam that cut a hole in the spaceship, and climbed inside. As he entered, he got a message from FRIDAY.

"Boss, there's a call from Miss Potts."

Oh, no! Iron Man thought.

"But you said save the sorcerer!" Spider-Man shouted, then a moment later said, **"I can't breathe!"**

"Tony? Oh, my God! Are you all right? What's happening?!" Pepper said, sounding desperately worried. The attack on New York was in the news, and she knew he was involved.

"Yeah, I'm fine," Iron Man lied. "I just think we might need to re-arrange our 8:30 date."

"Why? Please tell me you're not on the ship," Pepper said urgently.

"I'm sorry. I'm sorry. I don't know what to say."

Iron Man was glad that FRIDAY lost contact at that moment. He needed to find Doctor Strange. He didn't know that Spider-Man had managed to shoot web lines to the ship. The teenager pulled himself toward the ship, and climbed inside some doors just before they closed.

Standing at the spaceship controls, Ebony Maw put the planet Titan as the ship's destination. He smiled. His father would be pleased. He was taking Doctor Strange to Titan, and Thanos would gain possession of the Time Stone. The ship took off into deep space.

"Oh, my God!" Spider-Man said, as he watched Earth disappear. "Why didn't I stay on the bus?"

A very long way below, Bruce Banner and Wong stood on the streets of Manhattan, surrounded by debris. They had watched as Doctor Strange and Spider-Man were pulled up to the spaceship, and now the ship had disappeared from the sky. Clearly, the worst had happened. Ebony Maw had succeeded, and the Time Stone was on its way to Thanos.

Seeing a cell phone lying on the street, Banner picked it up and opened it. He was amazed to see Steve Rogers's name—it was the phone Stark had taken out of his pocket. *I can call Cap*, he thought, and felt a bit more hopeful. He turned around to see Wong stepping inside a portal to the *Sanctum Sanctorum*.

"Where are you going?" Banner asked Wong.

"The Time Stone's been taken. I must guard the Sanctum. What will you do?"

Banner held up the phone. "I'm going to call someone."

To the Rescue

In a distant part of the galaxy, a spaceship was traveling between stars. Pop music was playing, and some of the ship's crew were singing. They called themselves the "Guardians of the Galaxy," and there were six of them, all very different.

Their leader, Peter Quill, who was the super hero Star-Lord, was at the controls of the ship. He had been taken from Earth as a child by alien criminals, and they had taught him many skills. Other powers had come from his alien father, Ego, but were lost after Ego's death. Governments had considered his team, the Guardians, to be criminals, but the group now did great work protecting the planets in their galaxy from attack. Sometimes, of course, they took something for themselves, too.

A short time ago, they had received a call for help, and were traveling to find out more.

Rocket yawned.

"Why are we doing this?" he asked. Rocket looked like a raccoon, but had advanced powers and abilities. With his partner, Groot—who came from a planet of creatures that looked half human and half tree—he had used these skills for criminal purposes.

"It's a call for help, Rocket. Someone could be dying," Gamora said.

"I know that, but why are we doing it?"

"Because we're nice. And maybe someone will give us a little something," Quill said.

"That's not why we're doing it," Gamora replied. Because of her past, it was important to her that the Guardians did good, not harm.

Quill said, "But if they don't pay us …"

"We'll take their ship," Drax replied in his deep voice. He had turned to a life of crime after Thanos had killed his wife and child.

"Exactly," added Rocket.

Worried, Gamora looked at Quill. He was her boyfriend, and she expected him to do the right thing, and make the team behave well. He gave her a look that said, "Don't worry."

"We're arriving," Mantis said. Mantis was a young alien woman who could read and change people's feelings.

"All right, Guardians, don't forget, this could be dangerous. Groot, put that thing away," Quill ordered.

Everyone turned to look at the last member of the team—Groot, a typical teenager, who had one tree-leg over his chair and was playing a video game.

"I am Groot!" the teenager said rudely. These were the only words that Groot ever said, but those who knew him understood what he meant.

"If you don't behave, I'll break that thing," Rocket threatened.

The spaceship started passing through dead bodies and large pieces of metal floating in space, and it slowed down. The Guardians didn't know it yet, but it was the *Statesman*'s call for help that they had heard. The team stared out of the windows in horror.

"What happened?" whispered Mantis.

"Oh, my God!" said Quill.

"I don't think we're going to get paid," Rocket said sadly.

BANG! A body hit the front window, and everyone shouted in fear. With difficulty, the team managed to get the man into the spaceship and onto a table. He was breathing but unconscious. He was also extremely heavy.

"How is this guy still alive?" Quill asked the question on everyone's mind.

"This is a very handsome, extremely strong man," Drax said admiringly.

"*I'm* strong," said Quill.

"You're joking, Quill," Rocket said. "Another sandwich and you'll be *fat*."

"It's true, you have put on a little weight," Drax agreed.

"He's anxious, angry, and very sad. He has lost a lot and feels a lot of guilt," interrupted Mantis. Her hand was on the man's head, and she was reading his mind.

Lifting his arm and gently feeling it, Gamora whispered, "It's like his arms are made of metal."

Quill had had enough. Gamora was his girlfriend, and he was jealous.

"Stop touching his arm. Wake him up!" he said.

Mantis leaned in and whispered a single word: "Wake!"

Immediately, the man roared, and threw himself off the table, breathing heavily. He turned around to find everyone except Groot pointing their weapons at him. The teenager was still playing his video game.

"Who *are* you people?" the man asked.

The crew gave him food, a spoon, and a blanket to put around his shoulders. As he ate, he and the crew members told each other their stories. They were amazed to hear that Thor was the Asgardian God of Thunder. Now they were able to understand the reason for his superhuman strength and his ability to stay alive in space. Thor explained that his world had been destroyed. Then, the warlord Thanos had attacked and destroyed the spaceship carrying many of the remaining Asgardians.

Some of the Guardians also had experience of Thanos.

"All the time I was with Thanos, he only had one goal," Gamora said. "He wanted to bring balance to the universe by destroying half of all life. He used to kill people, planet by planet."

"Including my own people," Drax said in a low voice.

"If he gets all six Infinity Stones, he can kill half the universe with a snap of his fingers—like this." Gamora snapped her fingers.

"You seem to know a lot about Thanos," Thor said curiously.

"Gamora is ... a daughter of Thanos," Drax said.

Thor stood up. This woman was the daughter of his greatest enemy!

"Your father killed my brother," he said angrily.

"Thanos *adopted* her!" Quill said quickly. "She hates him as much as you do."

Thor put a hand on Gamora's shoulder in sympathy. "Families can be very difficult. When I met my half-sister, she stabbed me in the eye, so … I had to kill her. It's life, isn't it? I feel your pain."

Seeing Thor's hand on Gamora's shoulder, Quill moved to stand between them. "And *I* feel your pain," he told Gamora. "I've really suffered, too. My father killed my mother, then I had to kill my father—"

Thor wasn't listening. "I need a hammer, not a spoon," he said, throwing his spoon over his shoulder. Noticing a space pod in a corner of the ship, he walked toward it, and started trying to work the machinery.

"How do I open this thing?" he demanded.

"Er, what are you doing?" asked Rocket.

"Taking your pod," Thor replied.

Quill stepped forward. "No, you're not," he said, in a much deeper voice than normal. "You're *not* taking *our* pod today, sir."

"Are you making your voice deeper, Quill?" Rocket asked.

"No," Quill replied.

"You are. You're imitating the god-man," Drax accused him.

"No, I'm not."

"He just did it again," said Mantis, astonished.

"This is my voice," Quill said, still speaking in the same deep voice.

"Are you laughing at me?" asked Thor, standing face-to-face with Quill.

"Enough!" Gamora shouted. "We need to stop Thanos. So, we need to find out where he's going next."

"Knowhere," Thor said confidently.

"He *must* be going *some*where," said Mantis, misunderstanding him.

"No, no. Knowhere is a place," Quill said in his normal voice. "We've been there, it's horrible." He saw that Thor was looking through their food store. "Excuse me, that's our food," he said.

"Not anymore," replied Thor.

"Thor, why would he go to Knowhere?" Gamora asked.

Thor explained that for years, the Reality Stone had been kept safe there with a man called the Collector.

"If it's with the Collector, it's not safe," Quill said. "Only a fool would give that man a Stone."

"How do you know Thanos isn't trying to find one of the *other* Stones?" Gamora asked.

By now, Thor had finished taking food from the store, and he explained more. "There are six Stones. Thanos already has the Power Stone. He stole it last week when he killed the people of Xandar."

The Guardians looked astonished. This was terrible news to them—they knew Xandar well.

"He stole the Space Stone from me when he destroyed my ship. The Time and Mind Stones are safe on Earth with the Avengers," Thor continued.

"The Avengers?" Quill repeated, confused.

"Earth's greatest heroes," Thor told him. He explained that no one had ever seen the Soul Stone or knew where it was—even Thanos didn't know. So, he said, it was obvious that Thanos would go to Knowhere to get the Reality Stone. Thor looked around to make sure everyone understood his thinking. No one noticed how nervous Gamora had become when he mentioned the Soul Stone.

Gamora moved toward Quill. "Then we have to go to Knowhere now," she said.

"Wrong," Thor said quickly. "We have to go to Nidavellir."

"Nidavellir is real? Seriously? I mean, there are so many stories about it," Rocket cried, jumping onto a table in his excitement. "They make the most powerful, terrible weapons you can imagine."

"The rabbit is correct and clearly the smartest of you all," said Thor, amused by Rocket's excitement.

"Rabbit?" said Rocket, insulted.

"Only Eitri, the king of Nidavellir, can make me the weapon I need," Thor continued. While he was talking, he had packed a bag with supplies.

"That's *my* bag," said Quill, "and this is *my* ship. And I'm not going to ..." He couldn't remember the name of the planet. A thought came to him. "Wait, what kind of weapon are we talking about here?"

"A weapon that can kill Thanos," Thor replied.

Quill's mouth fell open. "Don't you think we should *all* have a weapon like that?" he asked.

"No, your minds and bodies are too weak. It would kill you—you'd go crazy," said Thor.

"Is it strange that I want the weapon even more now?" Rocket asked.

"A little, yes," replied Thor.

Gamora had heard enough. "If we don't go to Knowhere, and Thanos gets another Stone, he'll be too powerful to stop," she said.

"He already is," Thor replied, thinking of what had happened on the *Statesman*.

Rocket had a plan. "We have two ships. So, Groot and I go with the big guy, and the others go to Knowhere to try and stop Thanos. O.K.?"

"O.K.," Thor said with a big smile. He liked Rocket.

He entered the pod, and Rocket and Groot followed him. Groot was still playing his game.

"Put that game down, Groot. It'll damage your brain," Rocket said.

"Goodbye and good luck," said Thor to the Guardians in the main part of the ship.

Now there were two teams, traveling to different destinations.

On planet Earth, in the city of Edinburgh in Scotland, a man with a yellow Stone in his head opened the curtains of his hotel room, and looked out into the dark night.

With Vision was Wanda Maximoff, Scarlet Witch. As her name suggested, she had long, red hair. She was from Sokovia, an Eastern European country, and a criminal organization had given her superpowers. She was able to read minds, and move objects and people using her mental powers and energy from her hands. Both she and Vision were Avengers, but they were on opposite sides. Vision was on the side of Iron Man and the government. Wanda was with Steve Rogers's group, and was hiding from the law. But she and Vision had started feeling very attracted to each other, and were secretly spending time together. Recently, Vision had disconnected from Stark and his Avengers group, and he and Wanda had gone to Edinburgh.

There was a sudden, high sound. Vision put his hand on the Mind

Stone in his forehead, looking confused.

"Vis? Is it the Stone again?" asked Wanda, getting up and going to him.

"It seems to be speaking to me."

"What does it say?" Wanda asked. She gently took Vision's face in her hands. The android kissed her left hand, then pressed it to the shining Mind Stone.

"Tell me what *you* feel," he said, looking at her lovingly.

Red energy came from Wanda's hand as she put it in front of the Stone, and moved her fingers slightly.

"I just feel *you*," she said, looking at him with wide eyes.

The couple kissed.

Later that evening, they went for a walk, holding hands. While they were out in public, Vision changed his appearance to look human.

"There's a 10:00 A.M. train to Glasgow to give us more time to be together before you go back," Wanda said.

"I could miss that train," said Vision, turning to look at her hopefully.

"There's one at eleven."

"Suppose that this time, I don't go back," Vision said, smiling.

"You promised Stark."

"I'd prefer to promise *you*."

"I could miss that train," said Vision, turning to look at her hopefully.

But Wanda was worried. "There are people who are expecting me, too. We both made promises."

Vision put his hands on Wanda's shoulders, looking very serious.

"Wanda, for two years we've stolen these moments together. We've tried to see if our relationship can work, and ..." He took a deep breath. He was an android, but he felt as if he was becoming more and more human. His feelings for Wanda were getting stronger all the time. *Is this what humans feel like when they're in love?* he wondered. He felt very nervous as he continued talking. "I, I ... I think ..."

"It works." Wanda finished his sentence.

"Yes, it works. So stay. Stay with me," Vision whispered.

But Wanda had seen something on a television in a small shop. She moved to get a closer look, and Vision followed her. On the T.V. screen were pictures of New York, showing a spaceship, and Ebony Maw and Cull Obsidian. The announcer reported that Tony Stark was missing.

"What *are* those creatures?" Wanda asked fearfully.

Vision knew the answer. His fears had become a reality. He sighed deeply.

"This is what the Stone was warning me about," he said. He took Wanda's hand and kissed it. "I have to go."

"No, Vision. If that's true ... then maybe going isn't the best idea."

"Wanda, I—" Vision answered, then screamed as a spear passed through his chest.

"*Aaaah!*" Corvus Glaive roared from behind him. He lifted Vision into the air on his blade, and threw him to the ground. The android's human appearance disappeared, and his skin turned red. His clothes changed to a tight, green, gold, and red suit.

"Vision!" cried Wanda.

Red energy came from her hands as she prepared to attack. But another Child of Thanos had appeared. Using a three-pointed spear that shone with blue energy, Proxima Midnight blasted Scarlet Witch across the street and through a window.

Corvus Glaive pulled his blade out of Vision's chest, then stood over him, his foot on the android's body. He dug the blade into Vision's forehead, trying to remove the Mind Stone. The android screamed.

Suddenly, a powerful force raised Corvus Glaive and Proxima Midnight, and threw them to the ground. Scarlet Witch was firing energy at them from the broken window. She lifted Vision into the air, and flew with him to a quiet side street. Leaning against a wall, the android looked at her with his clear, blue eyes.

"My systems are failing," he said, struggling to breathe.

Moving her hands over the long wound in Vision's chest, Scarlet Witch pulled the edges of the wound together.

Vision tried to smile. "Why didn't we just … stay in bed?" he joked.

There was no safety. Corvus Glaive appeared, followed by Proxima Midnight. Pushing Scarlet Witch away, the alien lifted Vision high into the air, and pressed him against a wall.

"Give me the Stone and she lives," he said.

Calling up all his strength, Vision flew with Corvus Glaive high across the street and onto the roof of a church. He fired a beam from the Mind Stone at the alien. But Corvus Glaive fired it back at him, and again the android was pressed against a wall. Again, Corvus Glaive tried to remove the Mind Stone, and again, the android screamed.

Scarlet Witch and Proxima Midnight were fighting again, and it wasn't going well for Scarlet Witch. But hearing Vision's screams, she found new strength. She fired energy at the alien, throwing her across the road, and flew up to him. Blasting Corvus Glaive away, she carried Vision through the air. But a stream of energy from Proxima Midnight sent the couple crashing through the glass roof of Edinburgh's main train station, down to the ground below. Vision tried to get up, but was too badly injured.

"You have to get up—we have to go!" begged Scarlet Witch.

Vision shook his head. "Please. Please leave," he said.

He was desperately afraid that the woman he loved would die with him. But she wouldn't go. Corvus Glaive and Proxima Midnight crashed through the station roof, and landed near them. Seeing Vision lying on the ground, their expressions became even more cruel as they walked toward the couple.

At that moment, a train passed through the station very fast. Proxima

Midnight looked puzzled, sensing something unusual. Then, she understood why. After the train had gone, a dark figure appeared on the platform opposite them. The man's face couldn't be seen, but his body was very powerful, and he looked ready to fight. Proxima Midnight threw her spear at him, but he easily caught it. He stepped forward, and now his bearded face could be clearly seen. It was Captain America.

Steve Rogers had gained superhuman powers when he had been given a Super Soldier Serum by the U.S. government during World War II. He had helped the government to win the war, and had become famous, and greatly loved by his country. Then, a plane he was traveling in crashed in the Arctic. He had spent sixty-six years unconscious, frozen in ice. Finally, his body was discovered, and he was brought back to life. He became a super hero again, and was the first Avenger. Seeing him now, Scarlet Witch and Vision felt real hope. With Captain America's help, perhaps they could escape.

Proxima Midnight was still staring at Captain America when someone attacked her from behind, and threw her through a café window. It was Falcon, whose real name was Sam Wilson. The super hero had flown into the station using his specially designed flight pack. He had been trained to fight in the air, and was a member of Captain America's Avengers group. Moving fast, he turned and fired on Corvus Glaive.

Captain America threw Proxima Midnight's weapon to a blond woman dressed in black, who was running toward Glaive. Black Widow's real name was Natasha Romanoff. She was a highly trained fighter, and she caught the weapon without stopping, then stabbed Corvus Glaive in the

stomach. She kicked him, and he fell backward.

But Proxima Midnight lifted a hand, and her spear returned to her. The two women began fighting, and Captain America joined them. Then, Falcon dived at Proxima Midnight, throwing her near Corvus Glaive, who was lying on the ground. He pointed his guns at the aliens. The Avengers had won, it seemed.

"Get up," Proxima Midnight ordered Corvus Glaive in her deep voice.

"I can't," Corvus Glaive answered weakly.

"We don't want to kill you, but we will," said Black Widow.

"You'll never get the chance again," Proxima Midnight replied. A beam of light shone down on the aliens, and they disappeared. Their spaceship took off into the night sky. The Avengers felt cheated—they had been so near to killing Thanos's powerful fighters. But at least they had succeeded in saving Vison. Now, helped by Wanda and Falcon, the android managed to stand.

"Thank you, Captain," he said gratefully. He and Captain America looked at each other for a long moment. They were on opposite sides of the law, but that didn't matter anymore. They were fighting for something much bigger than themselves.

"Let's get you on the jet," Captain America said.

The Avengers had arrived in a Quinjet, one of the technologically advanced jets belonging to the team. It was near the station, and the group climbed into it.

"Where to, Cap?" asked Falcon, who was at the controls.

"Home," said Captain America.

Captain America threw Proxima Midnight's weapon to a blond woman dressed in black, who was running toward Glaive.

The Promise

Inside her home, a little girl with long, red hair and green skin was crying in her mother's arms. Both mother and child were shaking with fear.

"Shhh! We'll be safe!" the woman said, covering her daughter's mouth.

Gamora and her mother were hiding from the soldiers on the street outside. There were terrible sounds of screaming and gunfire. Thanos's army was on the planet Zen-Whoberi, and his soldiers were killing men, women, and children. The Zehoberei had heard of the warlord Thanos, but had never imagined that his army would come to their peaceful planet. There was an explosion, and the little girl screamed. Moments later, the door was kicked open, and mother and child were dragged from their home.

Outside, spaceships and jets hung above the road, and bombs were falling. People ran from the soldiers, desperate to escape. Most of them had been divided into two groups, one on each side of the street, and Ebony Maw was speaking to them.

"Zehoberei … Choose a group, or die."

A soldier pulled Gamora from her mother's arms, and dragged her through the crowds.

"Mother! Where's my mother?" the little girl cried, hitting the man repeatedly.

Surprised, he dropped her arm, and left. The child turned, and found herself facing an enormous armored figure. It was Thanos.

"What's wrong, little one?" he asked.

"My mother. Where's my mother?" Gamora asked angrily.

He bent down to talk to her. "What's your name?"

"Gamora," she answered, unafraid.

"What a fighter you are, Gamora. Come. Let me help you."

He put his great hand out to her. She looked at him, unsure if she could trust him, then wrapped her little fingers around one of his. He led her down the street and bent down again so he was at her level. Then, he showed her a small, jeweled knife with two blades, one at each end.

"Look, it's pretty, isn't it?" he said, balancing it on one finger. "It's perfectly balanced. Everything should be like that. Now you try."

The child took the knife, and put it on her finger.

Outside, Ebony Maw spoke to one of the groups lining the street.

"Go in peace, and meet your maker."

The soldiers fired, and everyone in the group fell to the ground. The people on the other side of the street screamed in horror. They hadn't been killed, but many of their loved ones had. Gamora tried to look, but Thanos turned her face back to his.

"Concentrate." He looked at the knife, balanced on her finger. "Well done—you've done it!"

As he spoke, Thanos decided he would adopt this child. Perhaps he knew, even then, that she would be the child he loved most.

On the Guardians of the Galaxy spaceship, Gamora was playing with the knife that Thanos had given her years ago. Quill was wondering if he should hang more weapons on his belt.

"I need to ask you to do something for me, Peter," Gamora said, looking very serious. She had thought about this request for a long time, praying that she would never have to ask for help. But the moment had arrived.

"Yes, what is it?" Quill asked.

"We're going to fight Thanos—that's certain," Gamora said. "If things go wrong ... If Thanos gets me ... I want you to promise me ... you'll kill me."

Quill couldn't believe he had heard his girlfriend correctly. "*What?*" he said.

"I know something that Thanos doesn't," she told him, and walked away so Quill couldn't see her face. "If he finds out, the whole universe is in danger."

"What do you know?" asked Quill, increasingly upset.

"If I tell you, *you'll* know, too," replied Gamora.

"If it's so important, *shouldn't* I know?" asked Quill.

"Only if you want to die," Gamora said, turning to look at Quill with tears in her eyes. She swallowed. "Swear to me, swear on your mother's life that you'll kill me if Thanos gets me."

Quill was silent, wondering what Gamora's secret could possibly be. She was ready to die to protect her secret from Thanos—and it was a terrible thing that she had asked Quill to do. He loved her, and felt trapped.

"O.K., O.K.," he whispered finally.

The ship had arrived at its destination, the distant planet Knowhere.

"This place looks empty," Star-Lord remarked, as they flew into a cave.

"I can see movement," Drax replied, looking at a screen.

The spaceship landed, and the Guardians climbed out. They walked into an enormous room full of large glass cases containing objects gathered by the Collector. Hearing voices, they hid behind some furniture. The Collector, a white-haired man in a fur cloak, was lying on the ground.

"I *know* you have the Reality Stone. Give it to me, and you will not suffer," said a deep voice.

The Guardians watched as Thanos placed a heavy boot on the Collector's chest, and the man groaned.

"I told you. I sold it. Why would I lie?"

"This is your last chance, fool. Where's the Stone?" Thanos said, pressing down more heavily.

In the shadows, Drax took a long knife out from his boot. "Today, he's going to pay for the deaths of my wife and daughter," he said. Eyes shining with hatred, he started moving toward the Titan.

"Drax!" Star-Lord whispered. "He doesn't have the Stone yet. We have to get the Stone first."

The two men started to struggle. Mantis, desperate to help, put her hand on Drax's head.

"Sleep," she said, and Drax fell to the ground with a loud crash. The Guardians quickly bent down so they couldn't be seen. Thanos turned and smiled slightly. He picked up the Collector, and threw him into a glass case, then started walking toward the Guardians' hiding place.

"O.K. Gamora, Mantis, you go right. I'm—" Star-Lord whispered.

But Gamora wasn't listening. She ran forward, jumped on some boxes, and from there jumped on Thanos, holding her sword. Thanos, ready for her, caught the blade, and broke it in half. Without stopping, Gamora stabbed him in the throat with the other half of the sword. Thanos's eyes widened in shock, and he groaned. Then, using her little jeweled knife, Gamora stabbed him in the chest. Her father looked down at the knife he remembered so well, and put his hand on it.

"Why?" he groaned, and fell heavily to the ground. Gamora started to cry. "Why you, daughter?"

He held his hand out to her, then laid his head on the ground as blood poured from his neck. Dropping her sword, Gamora knelt down, crying loudly. After all that had happened between them, she still loved her father.

"That was quick," Star-Lord said, amazed.

"Wonderful! Wonderful! Wonderful!" cried the Collector, clapping his hands.

"Is that sadness I sense in you, daughter?"

Gamora's mouth fell open in surprise. Her father's body lay on the floor, but his voice could still be heard all through the cave. Star-Lord raised his gun.

"In my heart, I knew you still cared," Thanos continued. "But no one ever knows for sure."

His body disappeared in front of them. A red mist was passing through the enormous room, and the room was changing. Now, many things were broken and on fire. The Collector waved goodbye as he disappeared.

"Reality is often disappointing," Thanos said.

Gamora turned to see her father walking toward her.

"I mean, it *was* disappointing," Thanos corrected himself. "Now ... reality can be whatever I want."

As he spoke, Thanos held up the Infinity Gauntlet, which had three Stones in it, including the shining, red Reality Stone. With horror, the Guardians realized what had happened. Thanos and his army had come to Knowhere, and destroyed most of it. The Titan had taken the Reality Stone from the Collector. Then, knowing that the Avengers or the Guardians would arrive, he had made a trap for them—he had changed reality.

Gamora's sadness changed to terrible hatred. "You knew I'd come."

"Of course. There's something we need to discuss, little one."

With a scream, the young woman bent to pick up her broken sword, but Thanos seized her, and held her in front of him.

"Thanos!" Drax roared, and ran at him.

But Thanos held up the Infinity Gauntlet, with the red Reality Stone shining brightly. Drax's body changed into small square stones that fell on the floor.

"Let her go! I told you to go *right*, Gamora," Star-Lord shouted, moving forward, and pointing his gun at Thanos.

The Titan put his head on one side. "Ah, the boyfriend."

"You let her go ..."

"Peter!" Gamora said desperately.

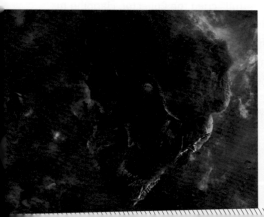

"... or I'm going to blow that great chin of yours off your face!"

"Peter ... not *him*," Gamora said, crying and breathing heavily.

Star-Lord looked confused for a moment. Then, he remembered.

"You promised. You promised," Gamora begged.

Star-Lord looked at the love of his life. He lowered his gun so that it pointed at her. His lips were moving, but no words came out.

"Oh, daughter. You expect too much from him. She's asked, hasn't she?" Thanos said to Star-Lord, pushing Gamora toward him. "Do it," the Titan said quietly.

Star-Lord didn't move. Thanos pushed Gamora again, and she screamed.

"Do it!" her father shouted.

Gamora was shaking violently, and Star-Lord's voice broke.

"I told you to go *right*," he shouted again.

"I love you more than anything," Gamora said, looking into his eyes and trying to smile.

"I love you, too," Star-Lord said, breathing fast. They both closed their eyes tight as he fired his gun. A stream of bubbles came out of it. Star-Lord's mouth opened in astonishment.

"I like you," Thanos said.

He raised the gauntlet, and transported himself away in a cloud of blue-black energy, taking Gamora with him. Drax's body returned to normal. Star-Lord, unable to fully understand what had happened, picked up Gamora's broken sword, his heart banging in his chest. Thanos had gone, taking Gamora with him. Where to? And what would happen to Gamora? He was desperately afraid for her.

Gamora's sadness changed to terrible hatred. "You knew I'd come."

Avengers — Together Again

In the Avengers building, in the north of New York state, a difficult situation had developed. Steve Rogers's Avengers group had arrived from Scotland on the Quinjet, bringing Vision and Wanda with them. For Thaddeus Ross, the U.S. government's secretary of state, it was simple—they were criminals. He had ordered James Rhodes, who worked for him, to call the police to take them away. But Rhodes hadn't obeyed his order.

"Rhodey," as people called Rhodes, was a close friend of Stark. He had become the super hero War Machine when he started using an armored suit created by his friend. He had fought with Stark against Earth's enemies and was an Avenger. The government used him to communicate with Stark and his Avengers group.

Rhodes knew that he would be punished for disobeying Ross, but he didn't care. No one knew where Iron Man was. Aliens had attacked New York, and the world needed every Avenger there was. Five of them were here now—it would be madness to put them in prison. He and Steve Rogers shook hands, glad to see each other. Then, Bruce Banner walked into the room; one more Avenger had arrived.

The group spent a long time talking about possible battle plans. There was one thing that they all agreed on—Thanos would return with an army, and he would find them.

"O.K., listen ... Thanos has the biggest army in the universe," Banner said. He was the only one in the group who had actually seen Thanos, and he wanted everyone to understand how dangerous the Titan was. "And he's not going to stop until ... he gets ... Vision's Stone."

The scientist hesitated over his last words. He had helped create Vision, and he cared about him. Thanos's fighters would find Vision again. If they succeeded in removing the Stone from Vision, it would kill him.

"We have to protect the Stone," Natasha said quickly.

"No, we have to destroy it," said Vision, who was standing by a window at a distance from everyone. The group turned to look at him.

"I've been thinking a lot about this thing in my head," he said, touching the yellow Stone. He walked toward Wanda, knowing that his next words would upset her. "I think if a powerful energy was aimed at the Stone—an energy very similar to the Stone—it could destroy it."

"Yes, and you, too. We're not having this conversation," Wanda said firmly.

"We *have* to destroy the Stone. It's the only way we can be certain Thanos won't get it." Vision whispered the words, talking to Wanda alone.

"That's too high a price to pay," Wanda said. There were tears in her eyes.

Vision, gentle as always, took her face in his hands. "Only you have the power to pay it," he told her.

Wanda walked away. He was telling her that it was her decision, and she felt terrible.

"Thanos threatens half the universe. One life cannot stand in the way of defeating him," Vision told the group, continuing his argument.

Looking down, Steve Rogers spoke. "But it *should*."

Banner entered the discussion. Because he had helped create Vision, he knew a lot about how the android had been built. He explained to the group that Vision's mind was made of many different parts. They were all mixed together and were all learning from each other.

"You're saying that Vision isn't just the Stone?" asked Wanda, hope in her eyes.

"I'm saying that if we take out the Stone, there's still a lot of Vision left. Maybe the best parts."

"Can we *do* that?" asked Natasha. She, too, began to feel hopeful.

"Not me, not here," Banner said regretfully.

"You'd better find someone fast," Rhodes warned. "Ross is going to come and get you soon."

"*I* know somewhere," Steve Rogers said.

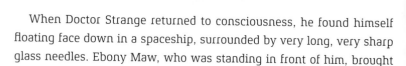

When Doctor Strange returned to consciousness, he found himself floating face down in a spaceship, surrounded by very long, very sharp glass needles. Ebony Maw, who was standing in front of him, brought his face very close.

"I've never failed Thanos," the ugly creature said. "If I reach Titan with the Time Stone still on you, there will be trouble."

Doctor Strange looked Ebony Maw steadily in the eyes. Some time ago, he had saved Earth from a magical attack that had attempted to destroy it. The sorcerer had suffered terribly, but he had succeeded in protecting the planet. To protect the Time Stone from Thanos, he was prepared to suffer again, and to die if necessary. Now, one of the needles started entering his face. It was extremely painful, and he couldn't stop himself groaning.

Doctor Strange looked Ebony Maw steadily in the eyes.

"Give ... me ... the Stone," Ebony Maw said.

Iron Man was watching in horror from above. He jumped when something touched him on the shoulder. It was Doctor Strange's cloak, and it was floating next to him. It looked like a real person, but with no head.

"You're a very loyal piece of clothing," Iron Man told the cloak.

"Yes, and uh ... speaking of loyalty ..." said a voice.

The super hero turned to see Spider-Man dropping down from above him.

"*What?* You should *not* be here!" Iron Man said, shocked and amazed.

"I was going home ... but it was such a long way down, and I thought of you ... and now I'm here in space."

"Yes. Exactly where I don't want you to be," Iron Man said angrily. Spider-Man was very young, and the super hero felt he had a duty to protect him.

"It's just ... you can't be Spider-Man and look after your neighborhood if there's no neighborhood."

Iron Man couldn't disagree. The teenager was right, but his life was in terrible danger. However, there was nothing Iron Man could do now to protect him. He led Spider-Man to a position where they could see Ebony Maw and Doctor Strange below. Behind them, the cloak appeared to be listening anxiously.

"See him down there," Iron Man said. "He's in trouble. What's your plan?"

Iron Man wants me to make a plan, Spider-Man thought excitedly. *Maybe I can help!* He thought quickly.

"O.K., O.K., ... did you ever see this really old movie, *Aliens*?"

Below, Doctor Strange started screaming loudly.

"Painful, aren't they?" Ebony Maw said. "Just one of them ..." Hearing a noise behind him, the alien turned to see Iron Man aiming blasts of energy at him from his gloves. Unafraid, the alien completed his sentence, "... could end your friend's life in a moment."

"I have to tell you, he's not really my friend. I'm saving his life because of professional politeness," Iron Man told him.

"You've saved nothing. And your powers are nothing compared to mine."

As he spoke, Ebony Maw raised his hands, and objects rose in the air beside him.

"Yeah, but the kid's seen more movies," Iron Man replied.

He fired a missile at the side of the ship, and it made a large hole. Things began to fly out of it, and Ebony Maw was pulled out, too. A moment later, the needles pulled away from Doctor Strange, who started moving fast through the air toward the hole. Seeing this, Spider-Man shot a web line at the sorcerer with one hand, while holding onto the ship with his other hand. But it didn't help, and Doctor Strange flew out of the ship. Just as this happened, four metal arms came out of Spider-Man's suit, and fixed themselves to the inside of the hole. The teenager was able to pull the sorcerer back inside.

"What are those?" Spider-Man cried. He hadn't realized that his space suit had arms.

Now that Doctor Strange was safely inside the ship, Iron Man fired beams at the hole to close it. The sorcerer fell heavily to the floor. Ebony Maw's frozen body floated away into space. It really *was* a little like what had happened in *Aliens*, Spider-Man thought. In the film, when a door was opened and the air pressure in the spaceship suddenly dropped, one of the aliens was pulled out into space. He felt very proud that his plan had succeeded. Together, he and Iron Man had managed to stop one of Thanos's most powerful fighters.

The cloak flew toward Spider-Man and "stood" next to him. The young hero put his hand out.

"Hey, we haven't met."

The cloak ignored him and moved toward Doctor Strange, who got up. Immediately, the cloak dropped onto the sorcerer's shoulders.

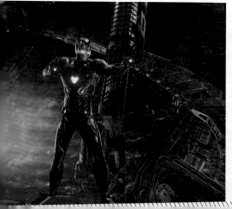

"We have to turn this ship back," Doctor Strange said to Stark, whose Iron Man suit had disappeared. "I want to protect the Stone."

"And I want you to thank me," Stark replied. He couldn't believe that the sorcerer wasn't more grateful to him.

"For what? Nearly sending me into space?"

"Who just saved your life? *Me*."

The two men faced each other.

"I seriously don't know how you fit your big head into that helmet," Doctor Strange said.

"Why didn't you take the Stone away when I told you to?" Stark replied.

"Because unlike everyone else in your life, I don't work for you."

"And that's why we're flying billions of miles away from Earth."

Spider-Man raised his hand. "*I'm* here to help, too."

"Quiet! The adults are talking," said Stark.

"I'm sorry, what's the relationship between you two?" inquired Doctor Strange, confused.

"I'm Peter. Um ... Spider-Man."

"I'm Doctor Strange."

Stark had checked the controls, and he said now, "This ship can fly itself."

"Can we control it and fly home?" Doctor Strange asked.

"I'm not sure we *should* fly home," Stark replied, who had been thinking about what to do next.

Doctor Strange thought this was crazy. "We must *not* bring the Time Stone to Thanos. I don't think you understand the situation."

"No, it's *you* who don't understand," Stark said.

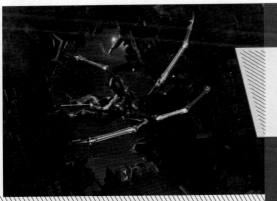

Just as this happened, four metal arms came out of Spider-Man's suit, and fixed themselves to the inside of the hole.

The two men faced each other angrily again.

"Thanos has been in my head for years," Stark continued. "Six years ago, he sent an army to New York and now he's *back!* I don't know what to do. So, I'm not sure if we should fight him on *our* ground or *his*. You know how dangerous he is. At least, if we go to him, he's not expecting it. So, I say we take the fight to *him*, Doctor. Do you agree?"

Doctor Strange, staring straight ahead, was thinking extremely fast, considering all the choices. He could see that there was a good reason for Stark's plan.

"All right, Stark," he replied. "We go to him. But you have to understand. If I have a choice—to save you, the kid, or the Time Stone, I won't hesitate to let you die. I can't, because the universe depends on it."

Doctor Strange had never been more serious. He hated the idea of making a choice like this, but it was possible he would have to.

"Nice. We've agreed then," Stark said, pleased. The sorcerer's words showed that he was a good man. He turned to Parker. "Kid, you're an Avenger now."

Peter Parker smiled, really pleased. His dream had come true—he was an Avenger. Then, he thought about what this meant. The Avengers were constantly risking their lives, and he understood why Stark had walked away so quickly. *I hope I have time to enjoy this*, he thought.

So, I say we take the fight to *him*, Doctor. Do you agree?"

The Price of Love

Gamora sat alone in a large room in *Sanctuary II,* wondering what Thanos would do with her. She felt very frightened. Her father appeared with a small dish of food.

"I thought you might be hungry," he said softly.

She took the dish, looked up at Thanos, then threw it with all her strength across the room.

"I hate this room, this ship. I hated my life," she whispered, turning away from him.

"You told me that. Every day. For almost twenty years."

"I was a child when you took me."

"I saved you."

Gamora turned to look at him, then shook her head. "No. No. We were happy on my home planet."

"It was a *crowded* planet. You went to bed hungry every night. There wasn't enough food for the whole population. I'm the one who stopped that. The children there have full stomachs now. It's a heaven."

Thanos spoke with great pride. But Gamora had never been afraid to argue with him.

"Because you murdered half the planet," she shouted now. "You're crazy!"

"Little one, think about it. The population is too great for the universe. A correction was needed."

The Titan spoke with absolute certainty. He was speaking from personal experience. All the life-forms on his home planet had died because of the overpopulation there.

"You don't know that!" Gamora shouted.

"I'm the only one who knows that ... and who will act on it." He looked at his favorite daughter, the one he was most proud of. "For a time, you believed in me, you fought by my side. Daughter."

"I'm *not* your daughter. Everything I hate about myself you taught me."

He stood high above her. "I made you the most feared woman in the galaxy. That's why I trusted you to find the Soul Stone."

"I'm sorry I disappointed you," Gamora replied.

Thanos sighed. "I *am* disappointed. But not because you didn't find it." The Titan touched his daughter's hair, then bent down so that his head was close to hers. "But because you *did*. And you *lied*."

He led Gamora to a prison cell. The enormous metal door lifted, and the young woman had a terrible shock when she walked inside. Her sister Nebula, who she loved, was hanging in the air, with guards on either side of her. Nebula was a Luphomoid, from a people who were similar to humans, with light blue and purple skin. Thanos had killed her family, and taken her as his daughter. He had trained her to be a killer, and added android parts to her body. Nebula had fought with Thanos against Gamora at first, but had then changed sides, and fought with her sister and the

Guardians. Now, her arms and legs were stretched out, and her body was pulled apart so her android parts were separated. Her head was shaking, and she was clearly in great pain.

"Nebula," Gamora said. She walked up to her sister, and touched a metal part. "Don't do this," she begged her father.

"Some time ago, Nebula secretly got onto this ship and tried to kill me. She nearly succeeded. So, I brought her here. To talk."

Thanos moved his hand inside the Infinity Gauntlet, and Nebula's body parts were pulled further apart. She started screaming, and her father watched with a cruel look on his face. Gamora, unable to bear her sister's screams, went to Thanos and put her hands on the gauntlet.

"Stop. Stop it. I swear to you on my life, I never found the Soul Stone," she said, crying.

Thanos waved a hand at a guard, who touched some controls. Nebula's voice spoke. "Memory files coming up."

A beam came from one of Nebula's eyes, and Gamora was astonished to see her own face appear in it. It was a memory from Nebula's past.

"You know what he's going to do. He's ready now to get the Stones. All of them," Nebula whispered.

Gamora's voice replied: "He can never get them all. I found the map to the Soul Stone and I burned it. I burned it."

Now, Gamora bent her head, unable to look at her father.

Thanos stood behind her. "You're strong. That comes from me. You're generous. That comes from me, too. But I never taught you to lie. That's

"You're strong. That comes from me. You're generous. That comes from me, too. But I never taught you to lie. That's why you're so bad at it."

why you're so bad at it."

He brought the Infinity Gauntlet next to Gamora's face. He was extremely angry, and had never sounded more threatening. "Where is the Soul Stone?"

Nebula shook her head, forming the word "No" with her mouth. She didn't want Gamora to tell their father, and was willing to suffer greatly, and even die.

For Gamora, both choices were terrible. When she didn't answer, Thanos closed his hand. Nebula screamed again and again as her body was stretched even further. Gamora couldn't bear it. She thought of all the people who would die if she told Thanos the truth, and tears came to her eyes. But ...

"Vormir!" she shouted.

Thanos opened his hand, and Nebula's body parts moved closer—but not quite together again. Nebula sighed as the pain—almost—stopped. Gamora went to her sister, and put her hand on her face.

"The Stone is on Vormir," she said in a low voice. She had only one hope now. Perhaps she could stop Thanos getting the Stone when they reached Vormir.

Thanos smiled. He had been sure she would tell him. "Show me," he said.

In the space pod traveling to Nidavellir, Thor was standing by a window, looking out. Groot wondered when they would arrive.

"You'll know when we're there," Thor replied. "Nidavellir is a star. There's a forge on it that uses its enormous energy. It's an extraordinary place. My hammer was made there."

He sat down, looking sad. His powerful hammer, Mjolnir, had been destroyed by his evil sister, Hela.

Rocket, who was sitting at the pod controls, realized that even the great God of Thunder might sometimes need comfort. He walked over to him.

"You lost your brother, too—that can be difficult," he said sympathetically.

"Well, he's been dead before, but this time I think it really might be true."

"And your sister and your dad?"

"Both dead."

"But you still have a mom."

"She was murdered."

"A best friend?"

"Stabbed through the heart."

Now, Rocket was really worried. "Are you sure you're O.K. to go to Nidavellir?" he asked gently.

Thor smiled, but seemed to be trying to persuade himself. "Of course. Anger, regret, loss, revenge ... these feelings make me want to go there. I have work to do—to kill Thanos."

"Yes, but this Thanos will be the most dangerous enemy we've ever fought."

"I'm getting a new hammer—don't forget that."

"It needs to be a *good* hammer."

Thor told Rocket more about himself. He was 1,500 years old. He had had many enemies, and he had killed them all.

"I'll kill Thanos, too," he said.

"And if you're wrong?" Rocket inquired.

"Well, if I'm wrong ... what more could I lose?"

Thor was very emotional, and there were tears in his one good eye.

"I could lose a lot. Me, I could lose *a lot*," Rocket said, looking serious. Feeling very sorry for Thor, he took something from a little bag that hung on his waist, and gave it to him. It was an artificial eyeball and worked like a normal eye.

"If you're going to kill that madman, you're going to need more than one eyeball. Take this," he said.

"Thank you, sweet Rabbit," Thor said gratefully.

"Hmm," Rocket said, still unhappy at being called a rabbit. Then, he added in surprise, "Hey, we're here!"

Groot watched with interest as Thor pushed the eyeball into his right eye.

"I don't think this thing works. Everything seems dark," Thor said, hitting his head to try to make the eyeball work.

"It's not the eye," Rocket said.

It was true. They had reached Nidavellir, and the star was completely

They had reached Nidavellir, and the star was completely dark.

dark. Three rings surrounded the planet, and were very close to it. People had lived on them. The rings usually moved around the star, but they were frozen, and weren't moving. Something terrible had happened—the star had died.

The pod flew through large pieces of machinery before finally landing on one of the rings. The team got out, and started walking through an enormous forge, full of large and very dirty machines. Groot was still playing his video game.

Thor shook his head, unable to believe his eyes. "This forge hasn't gone dark in centuries," he said.

"You said that Thanos had a gauntlet. Did it look like this?" Rocket said, pointing.

A short distance away was something that looked like an enormous glove. It was hollow and had shallow spaces for small, round objects. Looking at it, Thor had no doubt at all. It was a mold for the Infinity Gauntlet.

An enormous figure with long, untidy hair and a big, dark beard suddenly appeared behind them. The man threw Thor against a wall, then kicked Rocket and Groot into a wall of equipment. Four times as tall as Thor, he stood over him, with murder in his eyes.

"Eitri, wait! Stop!" shouted Thor. He had once saved Nidavellir's people, and knew Eitri well. Eitri was the keeper of the forge, and had made Thor's hammer. Now, his clothes were torn and dirty, and he looked ill and exhausted.

"Thor?" Eitri said, recognizing his friend.

"What happened here?" Thor asked.

"You were supposed to protect us," Eitri replied sorrowfully, then shouted his words: "*Asgard* was supposed to protect us!"

"Asgard is destroyed," Thor told him.

Eitri's anger disappeared as he realized that Thor and the Asgardians were in the same situation as the people of Nidavellir.

"The glove? What did you do?" Thor asked.

The enormous man sat down with a crash, and explained, shame and regret in his voice.

"Three hundred people lived on this ring. Thanos asked me to make a gauntlet—something that could use the power of the Infinity Stones. I thought if I made it, everyone would be safe. So, I made it. And then, he killed everyone—all except me." He held up his hands, and Thor saw that they were imprisoned in metal. "'Your life is yours,' Thanos told me. 'But your hands are mine.'"

Hearing this, Thor felt great sympathy. Eitri had had to make a terrible choice.

"Eitri, this isn't about your hands," he said. "All the weapons you've made—they're all in your head. I know it feels like there's no hope. Trust me, I know. But together, *you* and *I* can *kill* Thanos."

The God of Thunder meant every word.

Half a galaxy away, a technician had just finished fixing Nebula's body parts after the damage that Thanos had done. Nebula opened her eyes, and a metal piece around her left eye suddenly came out. The technician walked around to her head, and put it back. As soon as he had done this, Nebula hit him hard, and he fell to the ground. Then, she got free of the controls holding her in the air. Groaning and dragging one leg, she managed to walk to the computer in the cell. She typed in some numbers, and said, breathing hard, "Mantis, listen very carefully. I need you to meet me on Titan."

7

Love and Loss

Tony Stark was at the controls of Ebony Maw's spaceship, with Peter Parker by his side. The ship was approaching the planet Titan. The controls weren't made for human pilots, and the ship would be difficult to land. As they got near the ground, Parker realized they were going to hit an enormous piece of machinery.

"We might want to turn. Turn! Turn!" he shouted.

Stark turned the spaceship immediately, but its side hit the machinery, and the ship broke into several pieces. Luckily, the section that held the super heroes wasn't damaged. Doctor Strange quickly put a magical shield around them to protect them as they landed.

"Something's coming!" Spider-Man warned. He was hanging upside down from the ceiling of the spaceship, and his spider senses told him there was danger. As he spoke, a small explosive rolled toward them, and the three were thrown backward by the blast. They prepared for action.

Star-Lord, Drax, and Mantis appeared inside the ship.

"Die, Thanos!" Drax shouted. He threw another explosive at Doctor Strange, who put up a magical shield. The sorcerer's cloak flew toward Drax, and pulled him to the floor.

"Die, blanket of death!" cried Drax, fighting with the cloak.

Star-Lord pinned Iron Man against some equipment, but the super hero struggled free. He stood over Drax, and pointed a weapon at him. Spider-Man shot webbing at Mantis, so her arms were held against her body, but then Star-Lord kicked him away. The Guardian seized Spider-Man around his neck, and pointed his gun at him.

"All right, everybody, stay where you are ... relax!" Star-Lord said, as his helmet disappeared, showing his face. "I'm going to ask you this just once. Where's Gamora?"

Iron Man's helmet disappeared, too.

"And *I'm* going to ask *you*," he said, "—*who's* Gamora?"

"Tell me where the girl is, or I swear, I'm going to kill this kid," Star-Lord said.

"Let's do it," Iron Man replied. "You shoot *my* guy; I blast *him*."

He held his blaster against Drax's face.

"Oh, yeah? You don't want to tell me where she is?" Star-Lord shouted. "That's *fine*. I'll kill all three of you. And I'll beat the answer out of Thanos himself." He turned to Spider-Man. "I'll start with *you*."

"Wait," Doctor Strange said, puzzled. "Thanos? Who are you fighting for?"

Iron Man suddenly understood. "You're from Earth," he said.

"I'm not from Earth. I'm from Missouri," Star-Lord replied.

"Yeah, that's on Earth, you fool. Why are you fighting us?"

"So, you're *not* with Thanos?" Spider-Man asked, disappointed. Star-Lord's arm was still tight around his neck.

Star-Lord couldn't believe Spider-Man's question. "*With* Thanos?" he said, looking disgusted. "No, I'm here to *kill* Thanos. He took my girl—" And then, he, too, understood. "Who *are* you?" he demanded.

Spider-Man's helmet disappeared. "We're the Avengers, man," he said. It was a proud moment for him.

"Oh!" Star-Lord sighed.

"You're the ones Thor told us about!" Mantis said, wide-eyed.

"You know *Thor?*" Iron Man asked, astonished.

"Yes," Star-Lord answered. "Tall guy, not very good-looking."

"Where is he now?" Doctor Strange asked. Bruce Banner had said that Thanos had killed everyone on the spaceship, but Thor was still alive.

The sorcerer wondered how that had happened. He had a feeling that Thor would be very important in the fight against the madman from Titan.

In the forge on Nidavellir, Eitri took Thor, Rocket, and Groot to look at some machinery.

"It's a mold for a king's weapon," he said.

He explained that it was designed to be the greatest weapon in the history of Asgard, but it was never made. Its name was "Stormbreaker." It would increase the king's powers, strike with enormous force, and return to the king's hand—like Mjolnir—when it was called. It was even powerful enough to call the Bifrost.

"How do we make it?" asked Thor, very excited. With this weapon, perhaps they could race Thanos to Earth and stop him. But Eitri didn't believe it was possible to make it.

"You'd have to restart the forge. To do that, we'd need to wake the heart of a dying star."

The forge needed the energy of the star to work, and the star was almost dead. But Thor was a god, and nothing was going to stop him from making this weapon. An idea came to him.

Turning to Rocket, he ordered, "Rabbit, start the pod."

Something terrible had happened to Titan—both the Guardians and the Avengers could see that. Everything was in ruins. The planet wasn't quite in its normal position, and its gravity was not normal either.

The two groups had now agreed to work together, but they couldn't agree on a plan.

"We have one advantage," Tony Stark said. "Thanos is coming to *us*. We'll use it. All right, I have a plan. We trap him, we hold him down, we get what we need. We don't do anything else. We just want the gauntlet."

The plan was simple but would work, Stark thought.

Doctor Strange was floating just above the ground with his legs crossed.

Drax yawned.

"Are you yawning? In the middle of this? Huh? Did you hear what I said?" Stark said angrily.

"I stopped listening after you said, 'I have a plan,'" Drax replied.

"We don't have plans," Star-Lord explained.

"We just fight and win," Mantis said in her small, high voice.

Stark sighed. He was beginning to wonder if a plan was possible with these people.

"Mr. Star-Lord, can you tell your people to concentrate?" he asked.

"'Star-Lord' is fine," the Guardian replied. "I like your plan. But you should let *me* do the plan, that way it might be really good. Don't forget, I'm only half human. So that's 50% of me that's stupid. That's 100% of you."

They weren't making any progress.

Then, Mantis said, pointing to Doctor Strange, "Excuse me, but ... does your friend ... often *do* that?"

Everyone turned to look. Doctor Strange was floating just above the ground with his legs crossed. His hands were making strange movements, and the Time Stone was shining bright green. There was a green mist around him, and lines of energy going from the Stone to his arms, which had green rings around them. Behind him, his cloak was moving in the air. His eyes were closed. His head was moving from side to side very fast—he seemed to be watching something.

"Strange, are you all right?" Stark shouted, and walked toward him. The sorcerer's eyes opened, and he fell to the ground, shouting in fear and surprise.

"Hey, what was that?" Spider-Man asked.

"I went forward in time," Doctor Strange answered, breathing heavily. "I wanted to see all the different futures—all the possible results of the fight with Thanos."

"How many did you see?" Star-Lord asked.

"14,000,605," Doctor Strange replied.

Stark asked the question everyone was thinking. "How many did we win?"

Doctor Strange looked away. "One," he replied in a low voice.

Vormir was a planet of sand and shallow pools of water. Nothing lived there. An enormous sun hung above it, blocked by its moon. Only the edge of the sun could be seen. There was only one reason to visit it—to find the Soul Stone.

"If the Stone isn't there, your sister will pay," Thanos told Gamora.

They were walking across the sand toward a mountain, under a dark blue sky. There were paths up the mountain, and after many hours of walking, father and daughter finally reached the top. They came to a large hole in the rocks. At the edge of the hole, a floating figure the size of a

human appeared. Its clothes were long and torn, and its face was hidden.

"Welcome, Thanos, son of A'lars. Gamora, daughter of Thanos," the creature said in a low voice.

"You know us?" Thanos asked, surprised.

"I know all who travel here."

"Where is the Soul Stone?" the Titan asked, desperate to possess it.

"You should know," the voice said. "But you will pay a terrible price."

Thanos stepped forward. "I am prepared."

"We all think that at first. We are all wrong."

The creature came forward, too, and showed his face. It was the face of a dead man. The man was Johann Schmidt, "Red Skull." A long time ago, he had taken a substance that he hoped would give him special powers. It had done this, but had also changed his physical appearance terribly. He had tried to find the Tesseract with the aim of controlling the world, but Captain America had defeated him.

It was snowing now, and there was a strong wind. Red Skull led the father and daughter past a ruined building and between two towers to the edge of a high cliff.

"How do you know this place so well?" Thanos asked.

"A long, long time ago, I, too, tried to find the Stones. I even held one in my hand. But the Stone sent me here. I cannot leave. I can only guide others to something I cannot possess myself. The thing that you are looking for is in front of you. The thing that you fear is here, too."

"What's that?" Gamora asked, confused. Was he talking about the

"To take the Stone, you must lose the thing you love. A soul ... for a soul."

cliff? Or something that lay at the bottom? Did he expect them to climb down the cliff?

"The price that you will pay. The Soul Stone has a special place among the Infinity Stones. You could say it is wise."

"Tell me what it needs," Thanos said impatiently.

"It wants you to understand its power ... So, it demands something that will hurt you to give."

"What?" Thanos demanded.

"To take the Stone, you must lose the thing you love. A soul ... for a soul."

Thanos looked around, puzzled. What could he give? There was only Red Skull ... and Gamora. Then, he knew the answer.

Gamora began laughing. "All my life I dreamed of a day ... a moment when you got what you deserved. And I was always so disappointed." She looked up at Thanos, who was standing with his back to her. "You kill, and cause great pain, and you call it kindness. The universe has judged *you*. You asked it for a prize and it said no. You failed. And do you want to know why? Because you love *nothing*. *No* one."

Thanos turned around, tears on his face.

"Really? Tears?" Gamora said, with a strange smile. Thanos never cried.

"They're not for him," Red Skull said.

Turning to look at Red Skull, Gamora suddenly understood his meaning, and her smile went. Terror came instead. Her father walked toward her, and she moved backward, away from him.

"No," she said shakily. "This isn't love."

"Once, I did not achieve my purpose. I cannot do that again. Even for you." Thanos whispered the words.

The young woman thought fast. If she killed herself, then Thanos couldn't kill the person he loved most. And he wouldn't obtain the Soul Stone. She turned around, took out her little knife, and stabbed herself in the stomach. But when she opened her hands, expecting blood, to her astonishment, only bubbles came out. She had failed—she was still alive. All hope left her.

"I'm sorry, little one," Thanos said sorrowfully. He seized her arm, and dragged her to the edge of the cliff.

"No!" Gamora screamed.

She struggled to break free from him, knowing it was hopeless. He pushed her, and she fell backward over the cliff, screaming, and holding her hands out. Thanos watched, his mouth open as she fell. He had killed the one person in the universe that he loved. His daughter landed on the ground far below, her arms and legs spread out. She looked like a broken toy. With that, Thanos exchanged the soul he loved the most for the thing he desired most.

A great, bright light rose up from the two towers, and surrounded them. It was the energy of the Soul Stone. The Titan stood with his eyes tightly closed, unable to believe that he had murdered his daughter. The pain in his heart was like nothing he had ever felt before. Even in the heart of the most evil man in the universe, some goodness had remained. He had chosen to destroy it. He lost consciousness.

When he woke, he was lying in a shallow pool of water. He sat up slowly. Feeling something in his hand, he opened it. There was the Soul Stone. Its bright orange light shone in his eyes so he could hardly see. Gamora's death was worth it, Thanos thought. He repeated the words until he believed them.

Feeling something in his hand, he opened it. There was the Soul Stone.

The Battle of Wakanda

King T'Challa walked toward the Avengers' Quinjet as it came in to land on the edge of the Golden City, the capital of the African country Wakanda. With him were his guards, and Okoye, the leader of the Wakandan army.

Until recently, the world hadn't known that Wakanda was the most technologically advanced nation in the world, and that its kings had had superpowers for thousands of years. The Wakandans had used their technology—and the mountains and forests that surrounded the country—to hide their successes from other nations. After the death of his father, though, T'Challa had become the new king and the super hero Black Panther. He had opened his country to the rest of the world, and in the battles between the two Avengers groups he had fought on Iron Man's side.

Very recently, Steve Rogers had contacted T'Challa to ask for help. Rogers hoped that Wakanda's scientists could remove the Mind Stone from Vision without harming him. T'Challa had agreed without hesitation. But it was certain that Thanos and his army would find Vision and the Avengers, and Wakanda was also ready for battle. It wouldn't be an ordinary war. If Thanos defeated Wakanda, he wouldn't just destroy their country. This was a battle to save the universe.

"You said we were going to open Wakanda to the world, but I didn't expect this," Okoye told T'Challa as the Quinjet landed. Its doors opened, and the Avengers came out.

"It seems I'm always thanking you for something," Rogers said, as he and T'Challa shook hands. They had fought on opposite sides in the Avengers' battles, but the two men had great respect for each other.

As the group walked toward the government buildings, discussing battle plans, Rogers was pleased to see his old school friend, Bucky Barnes. They had a long history together. An evil organization had imprisoned Barnes, given him superhuman powers, and controlled his mind. He had lost an arm, and had been given a new one with fighting powers. The organization had used him in its battles, and he was known as Winter Soldier. Finally, though, Barnes had escaped. In Wakanda, scientists had helped him regain his mental health.

"How have you been, Buck?" Rogers asked, delighted to see him.

"Not bad, for the end of the world," Barnes answered, laughing. It was a joke, but there was a frightening truth behind it.

T'Challa took some of the group to a tower on the edge of the forest that surrounded the capital. The king's younger sister, Shuri, was responsible for much of Wakanda's technology, and she was waiting for them in her laboratory. Vision lay down on a table, and she quickly examined the Stone.

"The Stone is made of many different parts, and each part works separately, forming a web through the brain," she said.

"That's right," said Banner.

"Why didn't you just reprogram the parts to work together?" the princess asked.

"Because we didn't think of it," Banner replied, embarrassed.

"I'm sure you did your best," Shuri said sweetly.

"Can you remove the Stone safely?" Wanda asked.

"Yes, but it will take time. I need as long as you can give me," Shuri replied.

There was a sudden warning sound. An alien ship had hit the defense shield that covered the capital. It struck at great speed, and was immediately destroyed, but the war had begun.

The group in the tower watched as more ships landed in the forest, throwing up debris and trees that hit the shield. Captain America and Black Panther looked at each other. Would the shield hold against these attacks?

Vision got off the table. "It's too late. We need to destroy the Stone now," he said. He was prepared to lose his life, but his words were ignored.

"Vision, get back on the table," Natasha said.

"We will stop this army," Black Panther said, turning to leave.

"Wanda, as soon as the Stone's out of his head ... destroy it," Rogers ordered.

"I will," Wanda promised.

"Get everyone out of the city, and all defense forces ready," T'Challa ordered Okoye. He was prepared for a terrible battle. But Wakanda's army was extremely powerful, and he believed that with the help of the Avengers they could win. They *had* to win.

On Nidavellir, a battle of a completely different kind was starting. The space pod was flying beside one of the star's rings, and Thor was standing on the outside of the pod.

"I don't think you understand," said Rocket, who was at the controls. "These rings are enormous. If you want them to start moving, you need something much bigger to pull them."

Thor jumped from the pod to the ring. "I know what I'm doing," he replied.

He was holding a line that was connected to the pod. Now, he began to swing the pod around him, making Rocket scream. His movements got faster and faster. Then, he sent the pod away from the planet, so it pulled him behind it.

"Start the engines!" he roared.

Rocket started the engines, and the pod crossed the surface of the next ring, pulling Thor along it. It seemed certain that the pod would pull Thor off it. But the god, using his enormous strength, managed to dig his feet in, and stay on the ring. His aim was to break the ice that was stopping

A great light appeared as the star came to life again.

the rings from moving. If the rings started moving again, then the star would come back to life. Now, the ice began to make cracking sounds.

"More ... power ... Rabbit!" Thor shouted.

Thor roared in pain as Rocket obeyed his order. The ice cracked, and the rings started moving. A great light appeared as the star came to life again.

"Well done, boy," Eitri, who was in the forge, said quietly. He hadn't believed the star could come back to life. But he knew that if anyone could make it happen, it was Thor. The god had achieved the impossible.

Thor landed on the outside of the pod. Looking through the window at Rocket, he pointed at the astonishingly bright light. "*That's* Nidavellir!" he shouted.

Rocket stared. There was a piece of machinery around the star that looked liked an eye. The "eye" opened, and fired white-hot heat into the forge. But then, a piece of metal at the center broke, and the eye closed. The beam of energy disappeared.

"That's bad! There's an important part that's broken. With the eye closed, I can't heat the metal," Eitri said through the radio, desperately disappointed.

"How long will the metal take to heat?" Thor asked.

"A few minutes—maybe more. Why?"

The god stood up on the outside of the pod.

"I'm going to hold it open," he said.

"You'll die," Eitri told him.

"I'll die if I fight Thanos without Stormbreaker," Thor replied. He jumped from the pod all the way to the eye on the star.

In Wakanda, small open-topped planes were flying low over the flat land between the Golden City and the forest. They carried Wakandan fighters and most of the Avengers. War Machine and Falcon were flying above them. Bruce Banner was still unable to change into Hulk, but he used an armored, flying suit called Hulkbuster that Stark had made. He was inside it now, and was running beside the people carriers.

"Wow, this is great!" he shouted, delighted. "It's like being the Hulk without—" He fell on a rock, but got up, shouting, "I'm O.K., I'm O.K.!"

The defense shield protecting the city ended near the forest, and Proxima Midnight and Cull Obsidian were standing just outside it. Behind them, a line of very tall spaceships that looked like pointed towers stood in the forest.

Inside the shield, the people carriers dropped to the ground, and large numbers of Wakandan fighters climbed out. They were Jabari, a mountain people, and had weapons and shields that used advanced technology. Now, they lined up behind their leader, M'Baku, shouting war cries. Captain America, Black Panther, and Black Widow walked to the edge of the shield. Proxima Midnight and Cull Obsidian stood on the other side of it, just a few meters away.

"Where's your other friend?" Black Widow asked, referring to Corvus Glaive.

"If he's dead, you will pay for his life with yours. Thanos will have that Stone," Proxima Midnight replied in her low, cruel voice.

"That's not going to happen," Captain America said.

Black Panther added, "You are in Wakanda now. Thanos will have only dust and blood."

"Our fighters are prepared to die," Proxima Midnight replied. Life was cheap in Thanos's army.

She raised her sword with a shout, and the Wakandan fighters watched in astonishment as the spaceships behind her slowly rose in the air. The three super heroes returned to their positions in front of the army.

"Did they surrender?" asked Winter Soldier, who liked to joke.

"Not exactly," Captain America replied.

The doors of the spaceships opened, and great numbers of alien creatures climbed out. The Outriders looked like enormous insects. Each was the size of a large man, and ran on four legs, but could also stand up. Proxima Midnight brought her sword down, and the Outriders ran out of the forest toward the defense shield. The Avengers and the Wakandan army watched in horror as they attacked it with their extremely long, sharp teeth. Some of the creatures got through, but many were injured and died in the process.

"They're killing themselves," Okoye said, unable to believe her eyes.

Black Panther shouted a command, and his army and the Avengers began firing at the aliens. War Machine flew over a large group, dropping explosives.

Behind the defense shield, another group of Outriders began to run to the right of the battlefield. Seeing this, Banner radioed Captain America.

"Cap, if that group goes around us and gets behind us, there's nothing between them and Vision."

"Then we'd better keep them in front of us," Captain America replied.

"How do we do that?" Okoye asked Black Panther.

"We open the shield," the king replied. It was the last thing he wanted to do, but Vision had to be protected. If they opened part of the shield, the group would turn back, and go through the opening.

"On my signal, open North-West Section Seventeen," Black Panther radioed.

"Did you say, 'Open the shield,' my King?" a woman's voice asked nervously.

"When I give the signal, yes."

"This will be the end of Wakanda," M'Baku said sorrowfully to Okoye.

"Then it will be the greatest ending in history," Okoye replied.

Black Panther stepped in front of his army. "Wakanda forever!" he shouted.

With their leaders and super heroes at the front, the army began to run toward the shield.

"Now!" Black Panther shouted.

A section of the shield opened, and the Outriders poured through. The two armies met, and hand-to-hand fighting began.

Black Panther spoke into his radio. "How much longer, Shuri?"

"We've hardly begun," Shuri replied.

"Try and work faster," her brother said.

"Allfathers, give me strength," said Thor. He was standing in the middle of the eye.

"You understand, boy?" Eitri shouted. "You're going to take the full force of the star. It'll kill you." He thought Thor was crazy—extraordinarily brave, but completely crazy.

"Only if I die," Thor replied, breathing very deeply.

"Yes. That's what … killing you means," Eitri replied.

There were two levers on each side of Thor. He pulled on them, shouting because of the enormous effort needed to do this. Energy from

the star started pouring past him and into the forge. The machinery was working again.

"Hold it! Hold it, Thor!" Eitri shouted.

He went to an enormous pot, and watched as the metal bars inside started to melt. Then, he pulled a lever, and the melted metal started to pour into the Stormbreaker mold below. But Thor, still holding the lever, was getting increasingly burned as the star's energy rushed past him. Finally, it was too much, even for him, and he lost consciousness. The stream of energy from the star carried him all the way to the forge. He fell a long way before hitting the floor.

Groot looked up anxiously from his video game. Rocket landed the pod in the forge, and ran to Thor.

"Thor, say something. Come on, Thor, are you O.K.?" he begged.

Eitri pulled the red-hot mold onto the floor, and started hitting it with his metal hands to free the weapon.

"I think Thor's dying," Rocket said.

"He needs Stormbreaker! Where's the handle? Tree, help me find the handle?" Eitri shouted.

Slowly, Groot put down his video game. He looked at Eitri and saw the two parts of the weapon. He walked to them, and opened his left hand. His fingers started to grow, and they wrapped themselves around the two parts. Shouting in pain, he pushed the red-hot parts together so they became one. He lifted the weapon in the air. Then, shouting loudly,

A section of the shield opened, and the Outriders poured through. The two armies met, and hand-to-hand fighting began.

Shouting in pain, he pushed the white-hot parts together so they became one.

he hit his left arm, which held the weapon, with his right arm. Half of his left arm fell to the ground, its fingers around Stormbreaker, becoming a handle. The weapon rose in the air, light flashing from it. Thor was still lying on the floor, burned and unconscious—but his hand opened.

The battle against Thanos's army was going badly. Inside Hulkbuster, Banner jumped into the middle of the Outriders. Winter Soldier shot at them from the air, and Captain America and Black Panther fought together. The super heroes were killing as many of the creatures as they could, but for each super hero, there were seven aliens attacking them with their terrible teeth.

"There are too many of them! *Aaaah!*" Bruce Banner cried from inside his Hulkbuster suit.

War Machine was firing missiles at the aliens when Cull Obsidian's enormous hammer knocked him to the ground. Cull Obsidian and Proxima Midnight were walking through the battlefield, pleased that the battle was going so well. They didn't want to fail Thanos again.

Suddenly, there was a loud crash as a great beam of light came down from the sky, and hit the ground. Stormbreaker flew out of it, hitting Outriders at great speed as they ran from it. Light flashed from the weapon as it attacked the aliens around the super heroes. Then, it returned to its owner, Thor. The god had appeared in the beam of light with Rocket and Groot beside him. The light disappeared. On the battlefield, fighting stopped as everyone stared in astonishment.

Freed from his alien attackers, Bruce Banner laughed. "Hahaha! You guys are finished!" he shouted.

Proxima Midnight and Cull Obsidian watched fearfully as Thor ran forward, light pouring from Stormbreaker.

"Bring me Thanos!" he roared.

He jumped high in the air, eyes shining with light, surrounded by lightning. When he landed, he hit the ground with his weapon. The Outriders ran.

The god had appeared in the beam of light with Rocket and Groot beside him.

The Battle of Titan

Arriving on his home planet, Titan, Thanos knew immediately that his plans had gone wrong. The broken pieces of Ebony Maw's spaceship lay on the ground, but there was no sign of Ebony Maw.

"You must be Thanos," a voice said behind him.

The Titan turned to see Doctor Strange sitting on the steps of a ruined building. He didn't know that Star-Lord and Drax were hiding behind some rocks, and that Spider-Man was watching from another part of the ruin.

"Ebony Maw is dead, isn't he?" he asked.

"Yes," Doctor Strange answered.

"I'm sorry to hear that," Thanos said, sadness in his voice. He noticed a piece of jewelry around the man's neck, and immediately guessed that it held the Time Stone. *That will be mine soon*, he thought. "But he brought you here," Thanos said now. "Where do you think you are?"

"Let me guess. Your home?"

"It *was*."

Thanos closed his hand in the gauntlet, and a red light shone from the Reality Stone. Doctor Strange was astonished to see a beautiful city center appear behind Thanos. There were lovely green spaces, large pools, and technologically advanced buildings.

"My home was beautiful," Thanos said, lost in a dream of the past. "But Titan was like most places. Too many mouths and not enough food. We used everything on the planet—nothing was left. I offered a solution."

"Kill half the population."

"But my solution was not to choose who died. You could be rich or poor. They called me a madman and threw me out. But I was right. *Everyone* died."

He opened his hand in the gauntlet, and the planet returned to the present. The Reality Stone stopped shining.

"Congratulations," Doctor Strange said. "Now you'd like to murder trillions."

Thanos lifted his right hand, and snapped his fingers.

"With all six Stones, I could simply snap my fingers, and they would all die. I call that ... kindness," he said in a low voice.

The sorcerer started walking toward Thanos.

"And then what?" he asked. He understood now that he was dealing with a madman, and wanted to get as much information from Thanos as possible.

"I'd finally rest, and watch the sun rise on a grateful universe. You need great strength to do something like that."

As he spoke, Thanos thought of the daughter he had been forced to kill.

"I think you'll find that our strength is equal to yours," Doctor Strange said. He moved into a fighting position, creating energy circles.

Thanos, still lost in his memories, looked up in surprise. "*Our* strength?" he said.

An enormous piece of debris came down on top of him. Behind it was Iron Man.

"That was easy, Quill!" Iron Man shouted.

"Yes, if you just want to make him mad," Star-Lord replied, as he flew toward Thanos.

The group had finally agreed on a plan, and now they were putting it into action.

Using the Reality Stone, the Titan changed the debris into small creatures that flew away. He stood up, roaring with anger. Immediately,

Doctor Strange started creating portals. Star-Lord put an explosive behind Thanos, then disappeared through a portal, waving goodbye. The explosion threw Thanos to the ground. As he got up, Doctor Strange's cloak flew to Thanos. It wrapped itself around the gauntlet so he couldn't close his hand.

Spider-Man appeared through another portal. He began hitting Thanos repeatedly, disappearing through one portal and then reappearing through another. It was some minutes before Thanos managed to throw him to the ground.

"Insect!" he said.

He picked up the boy super hero, and threw him at Doctor Strange, and they both fell down. Immediately, an enormous explosion created by Iron Man covered the Titan with fire. But Thanos had succeeded in getting the cloak off the gauntlet. He sent the flames up in a stream of fire that carried Iron Man high into the air.

However, the super heroes had another surprise for the Titan. A small spaceship suddenly dropped down from the sky, and crashed into him. The ship's pilot jumped in front of him, holding an energy blade. It was Nebula.

"This is a surprise," Thanos said. He didn't care about her enough to wonder how she had escaped from her cell.

"It was a mistake not to kill me," Nebula said angrily.

"It would have been a waste of parts if I had," Thanos replied.

Doctor Strange opened a portal above his head, and Mantis dropped through it onto his shoulders.

They began fighting. Nebula struck her father with extraordinary strength. She had wanted to do this for so long, and it was very satisfying.

"Where's Gamora?" she demanded.

Thanos threw her to the ground.

It was time for the next part of the plan. Doctor Strange threw magical ropes that twisted around the Titan's hand, and tried to pull off the gauntlet. The other heroes all attacked him at the same time, holding him down. Doctor Strange opened a portal above Thanos's head, and Mantis dropped through it onto his shoulders. She put her hands on both sides of his head, using all her powers to make him lose consciousness.

"*Aaaah!*" Thanos roared, trying to mentally break free. Nothing like this had ever happened to him before. His eyes went white as he became half-conscious.

"Is he asleep? Keep holding him tight," Iron Man ordered.

"Be quick! He is very strong!" Mantis said. She was finding it very hard to keep Thanos, with his enormous mental powers, even half-conscious.

Iron Man and Spider-Man seized the gauntlet, and began to pull. Then, something happened that wasn't part of the plan: Star-Lord landed in front of Thanos.

"I thought you'd be harder to catch. Just so you know, this was *my* plan," he said, very pleased with himself. "Not so strong now, are you?" He brought his head close to the Titan. "Where is Gamora?" he demanded.

"My Gamora," Thanos groaned, showing his teeth.

"Where is she?" Star-Lord repeated threateningly.

"He is in great pain," Mantis said, feeling Thanos's sorrow in her own body.

"Good," Star-Lord said.

"He ... he ... feels great sorrow."

Hearing this, Nebula stared at Thanos.

"Gamora," she said, suddenly realizing what had happened to her sister.

Star-Lord's heart stood still. "What?" he asked, staring at Nebula.

"He took her to Vormir. He came back with the Soul Stone ... but *she* didn't."

Nebula swallowed, praying she was wrong.

As she spoke, Spider-Man and Iron Man were slowly pulling the gauntlet off Thanos's hand. They needed only a few more moments to get it off completely. Guessing what Star-Lord was going to do, Iron Man de-activated his helmet.

"O.K., Quill, you need to relax, understand?" he said, speaking fast.

The Guardian slowly turned to look at Thanos.

"Don't ... don't hit him, we've almost got this thing off!" Iron Man shouted desperately.

Star-Lord brought his face close to the Titan. "Tell me she's lying. Tell me you didn't do it!" he shouted. He knew that Gamora was Thanos's favorite child, and that the Titan had never harmed her.

"I ... had ... to." Thanos forced out the words.

Tears came to Star-Lord's eyes. "No, you didn't ... No, you didn't," he said quietly, his voice and heart breaking. He began hitting Thanos in the face with his gun, shouting crazily. Mantis's hands dropped from around Thanos's head. Iron Man ran to Star-Lord, and seized his arm, leaving just Spider-Man to pull off the gauntlet.

"Hey, stop! Stop! Stop! Hey, stop!" Iron Man cried.

"It's coming! It's coming!" Spider-Man shouted, as he got the fingers loose. "I have it ... I have it!"

At that moment, Thanos's eyes opened, and he realized what was happening. Just as the gauntlet was coming off his hand, he pulled it back on, and threw Mantis high in the air. Knowing she would hit the ground very hard, Spider-Man flew to catch her. The Titan kicked Drax into Star-Lord and Nebula, and all three fell to the ground. Then, he pulled hard on the ropes around his right hand, and threw Doctor Strange and Iron Man some distance away. The Guardians got up and ran toward him, but he blasted them with energy, and they fell down unconscious.

Iron Man flew in to attack him again, but Thanos hit him with his head, and he fell. There was a moon directly above them, and Thanos looked up at it. It was very close. Pointing the gauntlet at it, he sent an energy blast high into the sky. Iron Man watched, fearing the worst. Thanos brought his arm down fast. The surface of the moon was broken into pieces by the power of the blast, and enormous rocks crashed down on the super heroes.

In the laboratory, Vision lay on a table as Shuri worked to remove the Mind Stone. But progress was slow, and Scarlet Witch watched anxiously. Hearing a strange sound, she walked to the window. A long line of forest trees was falling to the ground, throwing up clouds of earth. Out of the dust, great war machines that looked like enormous wheels appeared, and rolled onto the battlefield. They were called Threshers, and could kill and destroy everything in their way. They moved quickly through the shield protecting the city.

"Move back! Move back now!" Black Panther radioed. These were some of the most dangerous things he had ever seen. War Machine and Falcon started firing at them from the air, but nothing stopped the machines from rolling forward.

In the middle of the battle, Black Widow and Okoye turned to see the Threshers' great wheels approaching fast. There was nowhere to run. They bent down, knowing that in seconds, the wheels would roll over them, and kill them.

Suddenly, Scarlet Witch landed near them. Her eyes shone red as she made a series of hand movements. The machines, flashing with red energy, flew up in the air and over the super heroes' heads. They landed on a group of Outriders, killing them immediately. Scarlet Witch turned to look at the two women, delighted she had saved them.

"Why was she not on the battlefield the whole time?" asked Okoye, astonished by Scarlet Witch's great powers.

They didn't know that Proxima Midnight was watching from another part of the battlefield. She had been waiting for Scarlet Witch to leave Vision's side.

"She's on the battlefield. Go in," she radioed.

Hearing this, Corvus Glaive went to Shuri's laboratory, and quickly killed the guard standing outside. Shuri turned off the computer system connected to Vision, and fired at Corvus Glaive. He easily threw both her and a second guard to the floor. But he hadn't expected Vision to jump on him from behind. The two crashed through the glass window, falling from the tower to the ground far below.

From the air, Falcon saw them fall, and radioed the Avengers to tell them. An Outrider jumped on him and he fell to the ground. Captain America was surrounded by the aliens, but hearing Falcon's message, he radioed, "Somebody get to Vision!"

Bruce Banner flew across the battlefield toward the base of the tower.

"I'm coming!" Scarlet Witch radioed, but Proxima Midnight, who had been waiting for the opportunity, attacked her. She fell to the ground, and the alien turned her on her back.

"Ebony Maw died alone. And so will you," she said in her evil voice.

"She's *not* alone," a voice said. Proxima Midnight turned to see Black Widow on one side of her and Okoye on the other.

"*Aaah!*" she shouted, unafraid. Jumping in the air, she attacked the two women.

On the edge of the forest, beneath the tower, Corvus Glaive kicked Vision, and he fell to the ground. Cull Obsidian was waiting with his hammer, and threw the android some meters away. The Children of Thanos stood over him as he slowly got to his feet.

Suddenly, Hulkbuster landed between them.

"This isn't going to be like New York, guys," Bruce Banner shouted from inside his armored suit. In New York, he had been unable to change into Hulk, and had felt very ashamed. Now, he had the chance to prove his fighting ability.

Cull Obsidan seized Hulkbuster's right arm. But Banner seized Cull Obsidian's hammer, and flew high in the air, taking the alien with him. They landed beside a stream that ran between high cliffs.

"Guys! Vision needs help *now!*" Banner radioed.

Then, the two enormous figures began hitting each other. Cull Obsidian succeeded in cutting off half of Hulkbuster's left arm, and Banner fell into the stream on his back. The alien stood over him, his weapon raised. Thinking fast, Banner seized the broken arm part, and held it up in front of him. Cull Obsidian hit it hard with his pointed weapon, and Banner hit the controls on the arm. It flew high into the air, taking Cull Obsidian with it. He hit the defense shield with a loud explosion. Inside his Hulkbuster armor, Banner sighed happily.

At the bottom of the tower, Corvus Glaive and Vision were struggling with each other. The alien, who was almost twice Vision's height, pushed his spear deep into Vision's chest, then seized him by the throat.

"I thought you were a fighting machine," Corvus Glaive said in his animal voice. "But you're dying, just like a man."

He pulled out his blade, and Vision fell to the ground. Corvus Glaive was ready to take the Mind Stone from the android's forehead, when someone ran into him from behind. It was Captain America.

"Get out of here!" Captain America shouted to Vision.

On the battlefield, after a hard fight, Proxima Midnight had thrown Black Widow to the ground. The alien's weapon was raised to kill the super hero when Scarlet Witch, still lying on the ground, lifted herself up. Red energy poured from her hands. Proxima Midnight flew into the air, and into the path of a Thresher. Some of her blue blood fell on Black Widow's face.

"That was horrible," Black Widow said, disgusted.

In the forest, Captain America knocked Corvus Glaive's spear from his hand. The alien wrapped his long fingers around the super hero's throat, and began to tighten them. Then, the end of his spear came out of the alien's chest, and he was lifted into the air on his own blade. Vision, standing behind him, was holding the spear. In Scotland, Corvus Glaive had done the same thing to him—this was the android's revenge. Exhausted, he dropped the dead alien on the ground, and fell on one knee. Captain America helped him up.

"I thought I told you to go," he said.

The rock fall from the moon had caused Titan's gravity to change again, and debris was flying around in the air. Mantis, Drax, and Star-Lord had been knocked unconscious by the rocks, and were flying around, too.

Spider-Man, who had no problem with the change in gravity, used web lines to fasten them to things that weren't moving.

Thanos pulled himself out of the debris. Then, Doctor Strange appeared opposite him on a large rock, and the two began fighting. Doctor Strange sent thin beams of energy toward Thanos that sent him high into the air. Thanos returned a blast of energy that Doctor Strange blocked with a star made of mirrors. Then, the sorcerer rose into the air. Multiple arms appeared around his body, and he split into dozens of tiny copies of himself. The little figures surrounded Thanos, and each one threw energy lines that wrapped around his arms and hands. But despite the lines, Thanos still had enough strength to close his hand in the gauntlet. The tiny figures disappeared, and only the real Doctor Strange remained. Thanos closed his hand again, and pulled Doctor Strange toward him. He seized the sorcerer by the throat.

"You're full of tricks," he told Doctor Strange. "But you never once used your greatest weapon."

He pulled the Eye of Agamotto off Doctor Strange's neck, and squeezed it. It broke into pieces, but there was no Stone inside.

"It's not the real Eye," he said, and threw Doctor Strange onto some rocks, knocking him unconscious. The Titan raised his gauntlet.

Just then, a small, blue disk flew into his open hand so he couldn't close it. Iron Man landed in front of him.

"If you throw another moon at me, I'm going to get really angry," the Avenger said. Even now, he could joke.

"Stark," Thanos said.

"You know me?" Iron Man asked, surprised.

"I do."

Wasting no more time, the super hero fired missiles at Thanos. Then, he flew at him and attacked, using his suit's great technological powers. But he couldn't match Thanos, who now had four Stones in his gauntlet. The super hero finally succeeded in scratching Thanos's face. The Titan felt his face—and there was blood on it. He smiled.

"All that for a drop of blood," he said, and threw Iron Man to the ground, hitting him repeatedly.

Iron Man managed to stand up. The two powerful figures fired streams of energy at each other that met in the middle. Thanos moved forward, pushing the super hero's energy back until he reached him. He pulled Iron Man's helmet off his head.

In a last attempt, Iron Man changed his right glove into a short sword, and tried to stab the Titan. But Thanos simply seized the sword, and pushed it through Iron Man's left side. For Iron Man, it seemed the end had come as Thanos pushed him backward to sit on a rock. The Titan bent down, and put his great hand on the super hero's head.

"You have my respect, Stark," he said gently, looking into Iron Man's eyes. "When I've finished, half of the people on Earth will still be alive." He stood up. The sword was still in Iron Man's side, and he was breathing heavily, with blood coming from his mouth. "I hope they remember you," Thanos said.

He put out his gauntleted hand, ready to kill the super hero. The Stones shone.

"Stop!" said a voice.

Thanos turned to see Doctor Strange, sitting up with difficulty.

In a last attempt, Iron Man changed his right glove into a short sword, and tried to stab the Titan.

"Let him live and I will give you the Stone," the sorcerer said in a shaky voice.

Thanos stared down at him, finding it hard to believe the sorcerer meant this.

"No tricks," he said.

Doctor Strange shook his head as Iron Man looked at him in astonishment.

"Don't!" Iron Man said.

Like Thanos, he couldn't understand why the sorcerer would do this. But Doctor Strange lifted his right hand, and seemed to reach out to take a star from the night sky. The beautiful, green Time Stone appeared, turning slowly in the air between his thumb and first finger. In the sky, the stars seemed brighter. Doctor Strange had hidden the Time Stone in a star.

Thanos held out both hands to the sorcerer, greedy for the prize. Doctor Strange looked at the Time Stone, thinking about everything that would happen as a result of his actions. Iron Man could only watch as the sorcerer sent the Stone floating toward Thanos. The Titan took it gently in his left hand, then dropped it into the thumb space on the gauntlet. He breathed deeply as its powerful energy ran through his body.

"Only one more Stone to find," he said.

As he spoke, gunfire hit his gauntlet. Star-Lord dived in from the sky, firing at him with both hands. But by the time Star-Lord crashed to the ground, Thanos had disappeared in a cloud of blue-black energy. The Guardian stood up, de-activating his helmet, and pointing his gun. He looked around, puzzled.

"Where is he?" he shouted.

Iron Man, although in a lot of pain, was repairing his wound, using his suit's advanced technology. He didn't reply.

"Did we just lose?" Star-Lord asked fearfully.

Iron Man turned to look at Doctor Strange. "Why did you do that?" he asked sadly. The keeper of the Time Stone had given the Stone to Thanos in exchange for his, Iron Man's, life. He couldn't understand it. What value did his small life have, compared with the value of the Time Stone?

Doctor Strange looked at him for a long moment. "We're in the Endgame now," he said.

Victory

It had taken time, but the arrival of Thor had changed events on the battlefield. The Wakandan fighters were beating their enemies. The leaders of Thanos's army had been killed. Thor was attacking and destroying the spaceships in the forest. The ships began to leave.

In the forest, Vision was sitting by a fallen tree with Wanda beside him.

"Are you O.K.?" she asked anxiously, putting her hand on his face.

Vision gave a sudden cry.

"What is it?" Wanda asked.

"He's here," Vision said in a low voice.

There was no need to say more. Captain America, who was with them, radioed, "Everyone, get here now. We have a new arrival."

Black Widow, Falcon, Black Panther, Okoye, and Banner in his Hulkbuster suit arrived almost immediately. The battle sounds had stopped—there was complete silence. Everyone stood looking up at the sky, sensing something strange in the atmosphere.

"What's happening?" said Black Widow.

The enormous figure of Thanos appeared in a cloud of blue-black energy. He was only a short distance away, and Vision and Wanda stared at him fearfully.

"Cap, that's him," Banner said.

The Titan started walking toward them. With five of the Infinity Stones in his gauntlet, he had complete confidence. Banner was the first of the super heroes to run at him. Using the power of the Stones, Thanos caused Banner to pass through him into a wall of rock.

Captain America was the next to run at the Titan. Before he even reached him, he was blasted away by blue energy. Then, Black Panther ran at him. Thanos picked him up by the throat, and threw him to the ground. Falcon attacked from the air, but his wings suddenly became soft, and he, too, fell to the ground.

Watching all this, Vision knew what he had to do. He raised himself to look at the woman he loved.

"Wanda, it's time," he said in a voice that he tried to stop shaking.

"No," Wanda answered, her voice shaking just as much. She turned away, and wouldn't look at him.

But Vision was desperate. "*They* can't stop him, but *we* can. Look at me. You have the power to destroy the Stone."

He took her hand and put it on his face. "You must do it, Wanda, please." There were tears in Wanda's eyes now. "We ... are ... out of time," he said.

Wanda didn't feel she could physically lift her hands. "I can't," she said.

"Yes, you can," Vision replied, wrapping both his hands around hers, and looking at her with enormous love. "You can. If he gets the Stone, half the universe will die. It's not fair. It shouldn't be you, but it is. It's all right." He looked deep into Wanda's eyes. "You could never hurt me. I just ... feel you."

Wanda—now Scarlet Witch—moved away from him with her hand out. The red energy in her open hand began to shine. She experienced terrible emotional pain as she began to send the energy that would destroy both the Stone and Vision. Tears streamed down her face, and her heart seemed to be breaking in two. Vision lifted his face a little, his mouth open, as the energy slowly began to melt the Stone.

Near them, more fighters had arrived. War Machine, Winter Soldier, Okoye, Black Widow, and Groot all ran at Thanos, one after another, and the Titan defeated each of them easily. Looking over her shoulder, Scarlet

Witch could see what was happening. In only a few minutes, Thanos would be beside them. She started firing energy from her left hand, too.

Captain America, who had recovered, jumped toward Thanos, sliding on his knees in front of him. He hit Thanos hard under the chin, then seized the gauntlet, and pulled hard. It was a battle of strength, and Thanos looked at him with respect. Then, he knocked him unconscious with his other hand.

The Avengers defeated, the Titan walked slowly toward Scarlet Witch and Vision. Scarlet Witch turned sideways, and used her left hand to fire energy at Thanos. With her right hand, she continued to fire energy at the Stone, which was very near cracking. The energy stream from her hands was extremely strong—even Thanos found it hard to fight. He held up his gauntlet to stop the energy from reaching him, and slowly began to approach them. He was almost there when Vision whispered, "I love you."

The android had lifted his face. He seemed to like the feeling of the red energy on it. His mouth and eyes opened wide, and then closed, and he looked peaceful. Cracks appeared in his face. Suddenly, the Stone broke, and an explosion of yellow energy burst from it and went above the trees.

Vision disappeared. Scarlet Witch threw herself on the ground, crying like a child. She had succeeded in destroying the Stone, but her great love, Vision, was gone forever.

Thanos walked toward her, breathing heavily.

"I understand, my child. Better than anyone," he said in a low voice.

Scarlet Witch turned sideways, and used her left hand to fire energy at Thanos.

"You could never understand," Scarlet Witch replied. She looked up at the terrible creature who had caused her to kill Vision. To her surprise, Thanos bent down and touched her hair.

"Today, I lost more than you know," he said. "But now is not the time to cry. Now is ... no time at all."

He walked a few steps to the edge of the forest, where he could see the Golden City. Then, he closed his hand in the gauntlet, using the energy of the Time Stone. A green circle appeared around his arm, and another appeared in front of his hand. He began to turn the circle very slowly to the left, and time started moving backward. The yellow energy of the Mind Stone came back down into the forest, and moved in to a central point. Vision reappeared, alive and conscious, kneeling in front of Thanos, with the Mind Stone in his forehead.

"No!" Scarlet Witch screamed as she realized what Thanos had done. She jumped to protect Vision, and Thanos pushed her roughly to the ground.

The Titan picked Vision up by his throat. Using two fingers, he dug the Stone out of Vision's forehead, which cracked all around it. Vision died immediately, and Thanos threw him away, broken.

The Titan moved the shining Stone over the single empty space on the back of the gauntlet, and dropped it in. For the first time since the universe began, the six Infinity Stones were connected. Their united energy poured through Thanos, and his body shook as he tried to contain it. He bent backward, opened his arms, and shouted.

At that moment, lightning hit the ground in front of him. Thor appeared in the sky, flying toward Thanos holding Stormbreaker. He threw the king's weapon at him. Thanos held out his gauntlet to stop the weapon from reaching him. But even the energy of all six Stones couldn't fight

its power. Stormbreaker landed in the center of Thanos's chest, and the Titan fell to his knees. Thor landed in front of him, and put his hand on Thanos's head.

"I told you that you'd die for your crimes," he said, thinking of the murders of his brother Loki and his friend Heimdall. He pushed the enormous weapon deeper into the Titan's chest. Thanos shouted as Thor looked deep in his eyes.

Through his pain, Thanos slowly whispered the words, "Mistake! You didn't ... You didn't cut off my head!"

Smiling evilly, he raised the gauntlet and snapped his fingers.

"No!" Thor roared.

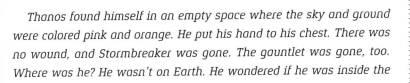

Thanos found himself in an empty space where the sky and ground were colored pink and orange. He put his hand to his chest. There was no wound, and Stormbreaker was gone. The gauntlet was gone, too. Where was he? He wasn't on Earth. He wondered if he was inside the Soul Stone. Was it possible?

In the distance was a small child. The child stood with her back to him, and he walked toward her.

"Daughter?" he said.

Gamora turned around. "Did you do it?" she asked in her sweet, young voice.

"Yes," he said, with great sadness.

The child just looked at him. "What did it cost?" she asked.

"Everything," he said, slowly shaking his head.

The child seemed to understand.

"What did it cost?" she asked.
"Everything," he said, slowly shaking his head.

The next moment, Thanos was standing in front of Thor, Stormbreaker in his chest. He stared at the gauntlet, which was smoking and black, and looked burned.

"What did you do?" Thor shouted, frightened. "What did you do?"

Thanos looked around. *Why should I stay?* he asked himself. He had achieved his great purpose. Finally, it was done. He brought his hand down hard, and transported himself away. Stormbreaker fell to the ground.

Captain America came out of the trees, with blood on his face, one hand pressed to an injury on the side of his body.

"Where did he go, Thor? Where did he go?" he asked urgently, looking around. Thor didn't reply.

Winter Soldier appeared at the edge of the trees, holding his weapon. He was looking at his arm, very puzzled—it was changing into ashes.

"Steve," he said unsteadily. A moment later, he fell to the ground, dropping his weapon. His body disappeared in a cloud of ashes.

Captain America walked to where his friend had fallen. He looked up at Thor, then touched the ground, trying to understand what had happened.

All over Wakanda, the same thing was happening. Fighters on the battlefield stared in disbelief as their friends disappeared, leaving only a cloud of ashes.

Okoye was lying on the ground when Black Panther came to her.

"Get up! This is no place to die," he said, and disappeared as he put out a hand to help her up. Okoye stared in horror.

In other parts of the forest, super heroes were dying.

Rocket and Groot were sitting together.

"I am Groot!" Groot said weakly.

"Oh, no!" Rocket's heart broke as his closest friend disappeared.

Wanda was sitting by Vision's dead body. She started disappearing, and lifted her head to the sky, smiling, glad to die.

Falcon, lying wounded on the ground, disappeared. Rhodey, who was searching for him, shouted "Sam! Sam!" desperately. Okoye could hear him shouting as she cried for her dead king.

On Titan, the super heroes were slowly getting to their feet, and beginning to walk around. Star-Lord, walking with difficulty, had his arm around Mantis's shoulders.

"Something's happening," Mantis said slowly, before changing into ashes and disappearing. Star-Lord's mouth fell open in astonishment. He looked around, and saw one of Drax's arms disappear, then another. Drax disappeared completely.

The Guardian stared around in horror. "Oh, no," he said as he, too, disappeared.

"Tony," said a voice behind Iron Man. He turned around.

It was Doctor Strange.

"There was no other way," the sorcerer said sadly, and disappeared.

"Mr. Stark? I don't feel so good," Spider-Man said, looking at his arm, sounding scared and very young.

"Are you all right?" Iron Man asked, trying to sound calm.

"I don't know what's happening ... I don't know what's happening." The teenager ran into Iron Man's arms, and began to cry. "I don't want to go, I don't want to, Mr. Stark, please, I don't want to go." He was quiet

"Oh, no," he said as he, too, disappeared.

for a moment, and then fell to the ground, Iron Man with him. "I'm sorry," the boy whispered as he disappeared.

Iron Man put out his hand to feel the space where Spider-Man had been. There was nothing now. He sat up, still looking at his hands.

"He did it," Nebula whispered.

Thanos had won.

Iron Man closed his eyes.

In Wakanda, the super heroes who were still alive—Captain America, Black Widow, Bruce Banner, War Machine, Rocket, and Thor—gathered around Vision's dead body.

"What is this? What's happening?" asked War Machine, confused and frightened.

No one replied.

Captain America was sitting on the ground, next to Vision's body. "Oh, God," he said, finally.

On a distant planet, the sun was rising. Thanos sat down at the entrance to a small hut, his body aching from his battles. He looked across at the sun on the other side of the lovely, green valley. It shone on his face, and he smiled, a smile of pure happiness.

Nick Fury and Maria Hill were driving along a busy New York street. For many years, Fury had been the head of S.H.I.E.L.D., a powerful U.S. government organization that protected the country and, later, Earth from attack. He had also been responsible for forming the Avengers group. At present, though, he was working unofficially. Maria Hill had been the second-in-command of S.H.I.E.L.D, but now she worked with Tony Stark's group of Avengers—and with Fury.

"Still no news from Stark?" Fury, who was in the driver's seat, asked now. They were desperate to find Stark and understand more about the alien attack on New York.

"Not yet," Hill replied. "We can't find him."

She checked her phone.

"What is it?" Nick asked.

"Something's happening in Wakanda," Hill said, looking at the screen.

"The same energy signals as New York?"

"Ten times bigger," Hill replied, then shouted, "Nick, Nick!" as a car suddenly crossed the street in front of them.

The other car crashed, and they got out of theirs to check on the passengers. But when Hill looked through the car window, there was no one inside.

Above them, they could hear, much too close, the sound of a helicopter. They looked up to see it crash into a tall building, and burst into flames. People screamed as parts of the machine fell to the ground. A motorbike lay in the middle of the road, but there was no rider near it.

"Call Control," Fury said urgently.

But Hill was suddenly feeling very strange. She looked down to see her hands disappearing. "Nick?" she said shakily.

Fury turned around and saw her become a cloud of ashes.

"Hill?" he said, unable to believe his eyes.

He turned back to their car, and a man disappeared in front of him. Something terrible was happening.

Fury took a pager out of his bag. He wished this was all a dream, but he knew it was real. It was an emergency. It was time to call for help.

As he held the pager with his right hand, Fury's left hand started turning to ashes.

"Oh, no!" he said as he disappeared.

The pager fell to the ground. Only half of it remained, but the word "Sending" appeared on the screen. Then, it was replaced by colored lights—and Captain Marvel's white star.

Activities

Chapters 1–2

Before you read

1 Look carefully at the front cover. Work in groups of three or four and discuss these questions.

a How many of the characters can you name?
b Choose two of the characters. What do you know about their past lives, and about their special powers?

2 Look at the Word List at the back of the book. Check the meanings of new words. Then answer these questions.

a What do these have in common? How are they different?

armor   *helmet*   *shield*

b What might a *sorcerer* pass through to get to another place?
c What do we call a creature that is not from Earth?
d Find four examples of *technology* in the Word List.

3 Read Who's Who? and the Introduction. Discuss these questions with another student.

a Which characters:
  • are or were kings?
  • were adopted?
b Which character is still a child?
c What are the Infinity Stones, and why does Thanos want them?
d What do you imagine Thanos wants to do exactly if he obtains all the Stones?
e How do you think the super heroes will try to stop Thanos from achieving his aim?
f What was considered especially good about the movie *Avengers: Infinity War?*

While you read

4 Complete the sentences. Write 1–2 words in each space.

 a Families from .... are on the *Statesman* because their planet has been destroyed.

 b The .... has fired at the *Statesman*, killing many on the spaceship.

 c Thanos tells Loki to give him either the .... or Thor's head.

 d Thanos .... Loki. Then, after Thanos leaves, the *Statesman* ....

 e When Doctor Strange and Wong look into a large hole, they see ....

 f Doctor Strange tells Stark that the universe is in ....

5 Answer each question using 1–3 words.

 a What important object does Doctor Strange possess?
 ....

 b What do the super heroes see hanging above a New York street?
 ....

 c Who leaves a school bus to help the super heroes?
 ....

 d What is Bruce Banner unable to do?
 ....

 e Who is Ebony Maw interested in?
 ....

 f How many super heroes are pulled up toward the spaceship?
 ....

 g What does Iron Man send to save Spider-Man?
 ....

 h How does Iron Man enter the spaceship?
 ....

After you read

6 Work with another student. Discuss these questions.

 a Why is Thanos so dangerous? Give reasons.

 b How and why did the Avengers break up?

 c What part does Tony Stark/Iron Man play in these chapters?

 d What is the situation on the spaceship at the end of Chapter 2?

7   Describe the importance of these to the story:

Vision   *the Bifrost*   *Steve Rogers*   *the Arc Reactor*

Chapters 3-4

Before you read

8   **Answer these questions. What do you think?**

   a What will happen on Ebony Maw's spaceship? Will the ship reach the Titan?

   b The title of Chapter 3 is "To the Rescue." Who do you think the rescuers are? Who needs rescuing and why?

While you read

9   **Match the sentence halves.**

   a The call for help that the Guardians received is ...   .
   b The Guardians rescue Thor, who thinks that ...   .
   c Even Thanos doesn't know ...   .
   d The king of Nidavellir can make ...   .
   e While Thor, Rocket, and Groot go to Nidavellir, ...
   f Vision and Wanda are in Edinburgh, ...
   g Captain America, Black Widow, and Falcon ...   .

   1 ... the other Guardians go to Knowhere.
   2 ... save Vision and Wanda from the Children of Thanos.
   3 ... Thanos will go to Knowhere for the Reality Stone.
   4 ... a weapon that can kill Thanos.
   5 ... from the *Statesman*.
   6 ... where the Soul Stone is.
   7 ... secretly spending time together.

10 **Are these sentences right (✔) or wrong (✗)?**

   a The Zehoberei are violent people. ◯
   b The soldiers divide people into two groups and kill one of them. ◯
   c Thanos decides to adopt Gamora. ◯
   d Gamora keeps a secret from her boyfriend. ◯
   e Gamora asks Quill to save her from Thanos. ◯

f Thanos changes reality before the Guardians reach Knowhere. ◯
g Star-Lord kills Gamora. ◯

After you read

11 Complete the sentences, giving as much detail from the story as possible.

   a Gamora says that Thanos has one goal. He wants to ...
   b Thanos liked Gamora as a child because ...
   c On Knowhere, Gamora uses her knife to ... and believes that ...
   d When Star-Lord fires his gun at Gamora, ...

12 Describe the personalities of Thor and Gamora, giving reasons for your descriptions from these chapters.

13 Discuss these questions with another student. Give reasons for your answers.

   a Which of the two couples are you most interested in?
   b Who do you think is the most powerful fighter in these chapters?
   c Do you think Quill was right to agree to kill Gamora?

Chapters 5–6

Before you read

14 Answer these questions. What do you think?

   a What will happen when Thor, Rocket, and Groot arrive on Nidavellir?
   b At the end of Chapter 3, Captain America says the Avengers will go home. Where is "home?" What will happen when they get there?
   c Why does Thanos take Gamora? What will happen to her?

While you read

15 Underline the incorrect word(s) in these sentences. Then write the correct word(s).

   a Rhodes doesn't obey the U.S. president's order. ....
   b The Avengers hope decide to remove the Stone—and destroy Vision. ....

c Spider-Man is pulled out of the spaceship and floats away. ....

d Iron Man and Doctor Strange agree to go to Earth. ....

e When Nebula starts crying, Gamora can't bear it. ....

f Gamora tells Thanos that the Soul Stone is on Earth. ....

g The star Nidavellir has died and its rings are burned. ....

h Eitri is the keeper of the rings and made Thor's hammer. ....

i Eitri thought he could save his people by making the Bifrost for Thanos. ....

After you read

16 Prove that these statements are true. Give details from the story.

a The U.S. government considers Steve Rogers's Avengers group to be criminals.

b The Avengers care about Vision.

c Thor is unhappy.

d Eitri is very angry and full of shame and regret.

17 Answer these questions.

a How does Doctor Strange show his bravery and honesty?

b How does Spider-Man show his bravery and cleverness?

c How does Rocket show that he can be kind?

d How does Thanos show his cruelty?

Chapters 7–8

Before you read

18 Discuss these questions with another student.

a Captain America says he knows a place where they can remove the Mind Stone from Vision. Where do you think this might be?

b What do you think will happen on the planets Vormir and Titan?

While you read

19 Who is speaking? Who—or what—are they speaking to?

a "Die, blanket of death!"

.... to ....

b "I'm here to *kill* Thanos. He took my girl."

.... to ....

c "... we'd need to wake the heart of a dying star."

.... to ....

d "How many did we win?"

.... to ....

e "To take the Stone, you must lose the thing you love."

.... to ....

f "I'm sorry, little one."

.... to ....

20 Underline the correct words in each sentence.

a Shuri will *destroy the Mind Stone / remove the Stone from Vision*.

b The alien ships attack the Golden City's *defense shield / walls*.

c Thor breaks the ice *in the forge / on the rings*, and the star comes to life again.

d Black Panther opens the shield to protect *Vision / his army*.

e The heat from the star melts the *ice in the forge / metal for Stormbreaker*.

f Thor nearly dies, *and Stormbreaker breaks / but Stormbreaker flies toward him*.

g Thor and Stormbreaker arrive *in Wakanda / on Titan*.

After you read

21 Answer these questions.

a Why does Thor decide to bring the star Nidavellir back to life?

b What is special about Wakanda?

c Why does Thanos's army come to Wakanda?

d What are Outriders and why are they so dangerous?

e How does Thor show that he is a god in these chapters?

22 Work with a partner and look back at Activity 19. Choose two of a–f and discuss where the speakers are and what they are talking about. Then have the conversations using your own words.

23 Discuss these questions with another student.

What are your feelings about the death of Gamora? Do you have any sympathy for Thanos? What is your opinion of him?

Chapters 9–10

Before you read

24 Discuss these questions with another student.

a Doctor Strange "had a feeling that Thor would be very important in the fight against the madman from Titan." How do you think Thor might be important?

b The title of Chapter 10 is "Victory." What do you think will happen?

While you read

25 Complete each sentence with 1–3 words.

a Thanos wanted to save his home by killing ....

b After he snaps his fingers, he hopes to ....

c The super heroes want to take Thanos's ....

d .... makes Thanos half-conscious.

e Nebula guesses that Thanos has ....

f Thanos wakes up after .... hits him.

g Rocks from a .... fall down on the super heroes.

h Scarlet Witch saves Black Widow and Okoye from ....

i Cull Obsidian dies when he hits the ....

j Vision kills Corvus Glaive by stabbing him through his ....

k Doctor Strange gives Thanos the Time Stone in exchange for ....

26 Are these sentences right (✓) or wrong (✗)?

a Thanos arrives in Wakanda and defeats some of the super heroes who attack him. ⬡

b Scarlet Witch destroys the Mind Stone and saves Vision. ⬡

c Thanos takes the Mind Stone from Vision, and kills him. ⬡

d Thor throws Stormbreaker at Thanos's head. ⬡

e Thanos, who now has all six Stones, snaps his fingers. ⬡

f Everyone on every planet turns to ash and disappears. ⬡
g On a distant planet, Thanos watches the sunrise and smiles. ⬡
h Nick Fury contacts Captain Marvel as he disappears. ⬡

After you read

27 Answer these questions.

  a Which actions show Thanos's great and increasing power in these chapters?

  b Star-Lord and Thor make great mistakes in these chapters. What are they, and what happens as a result?

  c Describe the part that Scarlet Witch plays in Chapter 10.

28 Work in pairs. Act out the conversation between Thanos and Doctor Strange when Thanos shows Doctor Strange his city from the past.

  Student A: You are Thanos. Tell Doctor Strange about Titan, its problem, and your solution.

  Student B: You are Doctor Strange. Respond to Thanos and ask an important question.

29 Discuss these questions with another student. Give reasons for your answers.

  a "With all six Stones, I could simply snap my fingers, and they would all die. I call that ... kindness."
  What do you think of Thanos's statement? Do you think Thanos is a madman? What are your feelings about him at the end of the story?

  b Why do you think Doctor Strange exchanged Iron Man's life for the Time Stone? How do you feel about this?

  c What is the meaning of the scene in Chapter 10 showing Gamora as a child?

  d How do you feel about these characters? Why?

  Star-Lord   Iron Man   Scarlet Witch   Vision   Thor

  e Do you think that Captain Marvel received Nick Fury's message? What might happen if she did?

  f How do you feel about the story, now that you have finished it?

Writing

30 You are a reporter. Write a report for television news about the attack on New York.

31 "Thanos is completely evil. But he is the reason that the book is so exciting." Do you agree? Give reasons for your opinions.

32 Describe the relationships between the two couples in the book and what happens to them. Which couple do you feel most for? Give reasons for your answers.

33 Write a book report. Describe what happens, and give your opinion of the book, with reasons.

34 "All the super heroes are very similar." Discuss this statement, and say which hero you like best. Give reasons for your opinions.

35 You are Iron Man. Write an email to Captain America after the end of the story. Explain how Doctor Strange saved your life. Describe your feelings about this and Thanos's victory. Write about your future plans.

36 You are a reporter. Write about an interview with one of the super heroes in the book just before the Battle of Wakanda.

37 What are your three favorite scenes in the book? Describe them, and say why you enjoyed them.

38 You are Pepper Potts. Write a page from your diary after your conversation with Iron Man while he was on Ebony Maw's spaceship.

39 Write a plan for a film about one or more of the super heroes who is alive at the end of the story.

Word List

adopt (v) to take someone else's child into your home and legally become his or her parent

advanced (adj) very modern

alien (n) in stories, a creature from another world

android (n) a machine that can do some of the work of a person, and is controlled by a computer. It looks human.

armor (n) metal or leather clothing that protects your body, worn by soldiers in battle

ash (n) the soft, gray powder that remains after something has been burned

astonish (v) to surprise or impress someone greatly

blast (n/v) a sudden, strong movement of energy. In this story, a **blaster** is a weapon.

bubble (n) a ball of air or gas in liquid

cliff (n) a large area of rock or a mountain with a very steep side, often at the edge of the sea or a river

cloak (n) a piece of clothing like a coat without sleeves that hangs loosely from your shoulders

crystal (n) rock that is clear, or a piece of it

debris (n) the pieces that are left after something has been destroyed, for example, in an accident or explosion

forge (n) a place where metal is heated and shaped into objects

galaxy (n) one of the large groups of stars that fills the universe

gauntlet (n) a strong, metal glove used for protection by soldiers in the past

gravity (n) the force that causes something to fall to the ground or to be attracted to another planet

groan (n) a long, deep sound that shows great pain or unhappiness

helmet (n) a strong, hard hat that protects the head

missile (n) a flying weapon that explodes

mold (n) a hollow container used to shape hot liquid material when it cools and becomes hard

pager (n) a small machine that you can carry in your pocket and that receives signals from a phone. It tells you when someone has sent you a message, or wants you to phone them—for example, by making a noise.

parachute (n) a piece of equipment fastened to people who jump out of planes, which makes them fall slowly and safely to the ground

pod (n) a part of a space vehicle that can be separated from the main part

portal (n) in this story, a gateway—created by magic or science—to another universe

raccoon (n) a small North American animal with gray fur and black rings around its tail

realm (n) a country ruled by a king or queen

roar (v) to shout something in a deep, powerful voice

serum (n) a liquid that is put into a person's blood, usually to fight infection or poison

shield (n) a wide piece of metal or other strong material used by police or fighters to protect themselves

sigh (v) to breathe out making a long sound, often when you are disappointed or sad

snap (v) to make a short, sharp noise by moving one of your fingers quickly against your thumb

sorcerer (n) a person in stories who uses magic

stab (v) to push a sharp object into someone or something

super (prefix/adj) in this story, more powerful

technology (n) new machines, equipment, and ways of doing things that are based on modern knowledge about science and computers

web (n) a net made by a spider to catch insects